Birnbaum's

Walt Disney World®

KID$

for

by kids

Wendy Lefkon
EDITOR

Cynthia Ambrose
ART DIRECTOR

Elisa Gallaro
SENIOR EDITOR

Deanna Caron
ASSISTANT EDITOR

Alexandra Mayes Birnbaum
CONSULTING EDITOR

HYPERION AND HEARST BUSINESS PUBLISHING, INC.

For Harris, the ultimate trooper.

ISBN: 1-56282-750-2

Printed in the United States of America

An enormous debt of gratitude is owed to Bob Mervine, Diane Hancock, Denny Artheim, Carolyn Bloodworth, Raquel Berberena, Mickey Metz, Dale Stafford, Mary Roche, Robin Casto, Debbie Salvi, Nancy Parent, Joel Curran, John Bender, Lisa Moye, Carole Munroe, Gene Duncan, Bob Desmond, Greg Taylor, Jean Cress, Karyn Esken, Paul Bosch, Jean Ambrose, Eileen Darwin, and Lucas Moore, all of whom performed above and beyond the call of duty to make the creation of this book possible.

To Phil Lengyel, Tom Elrod, Linda Warren, Bob Miller, and Charlie Ridgway, thank you for believing in this project and getting it off the ground.

And a personal thank you to Lois and Gil Spritzer, just because.

Other 1994 Birnbaum Travel Guides

Bahamas, and Turks & Caicos	London
Berlin	Los Angeles
Bermuda	Mexico
Boston	Miami & Fort Lauderdale
Canada	Montreal & Quebec City
Cancun, Cozumel, & Isla Mujeres	New Orleans
Caribbean	New York
Chicago	Paris
Disneyland	Portugal
Eastern Europe	Rome
Europe	San Francisco
Europe for Business Travelers	Santa Fe & Taos
France	South America
Germany	Spain
Great Britain	United States
Hawaii	USA for Business Travelers
Ireland	Walt Disney World
Italy	Washington, D.C.

CONTENTS

We Wrote This Book!

Finally kids have their very own guide to all the wonders of Walt Disney World.

This brand-new book was created for kids, by the kids you see in the photo above, and by the big kid in the front—that's me. As editor of *Birnbaum's Walt Disney World*, I have spent more hours than I can count at the three theme parks and all around the Walt Disney World resort. And, like the kids in this picture, I always wish I could stay a little longer.

The mail that pours into our office (from adults and kids) reminds me that kids love to help plan a Walt Disney World vacation, and that parents welcome their input. So what you'll read on the pages that follow is Walt Disney World from a kid's perspective. Since you won't have time to see everything, read the descriptions and decide which attractions you most want to see—and which you could live without. At the right and on the next page, we tell you a little bit about each of the kids who participated in this project. This will give you an idea of which opinions might most be like your own.

To write this book, we spent eight days touring the Magic Kingdom, Epcot Center, and the Disney-MGM Studios Theme Park. We visited Discovery Island, ate in a wide variety of restaurants, and stopped by many of the hotels on the Disney grounds. We all flew into Orlando on Delta Air Lines. We stayed at the Walt Disney World Dolphin, where we were treated a bit like royalty. "I felt like a queen in casual clothes," said one of our gang.

Robert Raack
Age 8

Robert, who previously helped write a book for a class project, is a second-grade student at Danebo Elementary School in Eugene, Oregon. He is very interested in dragons, and likes to play video games and soccer.

Taran Noah Smith
Age 9

Taran plays Mark Taylor, the youngest son on the hit show "Home Improvement." When he's not on the set, he attends the fourth grade at Marin Primary School in San Rafael, California. He likes to sail and ride his mountain bike.

Elisabeth Woodhams
Age 11

Lissy attends the Esperero Canyon Middle School in Tucson, Arizona, where she is in seventh grade. She plays the piano, is a member of her drama club, and enjoys horseback riding and swimming.

Ashley Pletz
Age 11

Ashley is a fifth-grade student at Hawthorne Scholastic Academy in Chicago, Illinois. She has worked on writing a book, *A Million Moms and Mine*. She also takes ballet lessons and has done some modeling.

Brian Leventhal
Age 12

Brian is a seventh-grade student at Finley Junior High School in Huntington, New York. He is studying cartoon art, and plays the clarinet in the school band. He also likes to swim.

Karyn Williams
Age 13

Karyn is an eighth-grade student at Robert E. Lee Middle School in College Park, Florida. She is an aspiring actress and recently appeared in a pilot for a television show, "Check It Out." Karyn also serves as a member of the Dolphin Youth Advisory Council.

David Bickel
Age 13

David is an eighth-grade student at St. John The Evangelist Catholic School in Hapeville, Georgia. He is a major sports fan and enjoys playing baseball and video games. His favorite teams are the Atlanta Braves and the Chicago Bulls.

Thomanita Booth
Age 14

Nita is a ninth-grade student at Indian River High School in Chesapeake, Virginia. She is a Mouseketeer on the "Mickey Mouse Club" show. Nita also enjoys singing in her church choir, ice skating, and going to the beach.

Of course, we didn't have time to see everything. All the kids agree that our eight-day stay wasn't long enough. If you really want to see all that Walt Disney World has to offer, the kids suggest you plan on one-and-a-half to two weeks.

The book is organized into five chapters. The first three cover the theme parks. We describe each attraction, and then the kids offer their opinions. The fourth chapter covers places like Discovery Island, the hotels, restaurants, and other activities and attractions not in the parks. The last chapter is filled with hot tips from the kids on how to make your vacation even better.

We can't wait to hear what you think about this guide. So please write to me with your tips for the best vacation in the World at:
Walt Disney World For Kids, By Kids;
60 East 42nd Street, Suite 2424;
New York, NY 10165.

Wendy Lefkon

The Magic Kingdom

The Magic Kingdom is probably the most special part of Walt Disney World. The soaring spires of Cinderella Castle, the odd-shaped white towers of Space Mountain, the carousel, the spinning teacups, and even the Dumbos flying through the air are the images that first come to mind when Walt Disney World is mentioned.

We spent two days (but we really needed three) exploring the seven "lands"—Main Street, Adventureland, Frontierland, Liberty Square, Fantasyland, Mickey's Starland, and Tomorrowland. The Magic Kingdom is packed with attractions, so it's important to plan ahead and set the order in which you will visit them. This chapter can help you decide which attractions you most want to see. Then make a list of the attractions that fall into your "second choice" category and a list of the things you can live without. That way you can organize your visit and avoid wasting a lot of time.

While you're in the Magic Kingdom, notice the little details that make the place so special. The theme of the lands is shown in the costumes worn by the people who work there, the design of the shops and restaurants, and even the design of the trash bins.

MAIN STREET, U.S.A.

This is the Disney version of how a small-town Main Street would have looked around the year 1900. And it's perfect down to the last detail. There are hitching posts where townspeople would have tied up their horses and many other touches that make this Main Street so attractive. Crews of painters keep the buildings looking fresh. They work their way up one side of the street and back down the other. Then they start all over again. There aren't any major attractions on Main Street, but the Walt Disney World Railroad begins its journey here. There also are a few other interesting things to see.

Walt Disney World Railroad

Walt Disney was a big train buff. He even built a model railroad in his backyard! The trains that run on the Walt Disney World Railroad are real locomotives that were originally built around 1900. They were used in Mexico, to carry sugarcane in the Yucatan Peninsula. That's where the Disney Imagineers found them in 1969. They have been completely overhauled, and all their parts have been replaced.

A ride on the railroad gives a quick overview of the Magic Kingdom. The full round trip takes about 15 minutes, but you can get on and off at any of the stations. Main Street is the starting point and ending point.

> "It gets you to different lands much faster than walking."
>
> —David (age 13)

In between, the trains make stops in Frontierland, Mickey's Starland, and Tomorrowland.

The kids agree that the train is a nice way to travel around the park. "I think it's a great way to get around without walking, and the sights are nice, too," says Karyn. David agrees. "It gets you to different lands much faster than walking."

Lissy thinks there should be a gate on the cars so young kids won't try to jump out.

What We Missed

Main Street, U.S.A. is lined with many different types of shops. There are places to buy candy, clothing, souvenirs, magic tricks, hats, cameras, jewelry, books. You can even get a haircut. Shopping hints are in the Everything Else in the World chapter.

Other attractions on Main Street that we didn't have time to see include the **Penny Arcade**, where you'll find today's video games plus lots of games from the early 1900s. There's an antique football game and machines that show the first motion pictures.

At the **Main Street Cinema**, you can take a break from the hot sun, rest your tired feet, and watch a few early Mickey Mouse cartoons. This is your chance to see *Steamboat Willie*, the first sound cartoon—and Mickey's first film appearance.

A variety of vehicles ride up and down Main Street during the day (especially when the park first opens). There's a bright-red fire engine, horse-drawn trolley cars, and others. You may be able to snag a ride on the fire engine if you get to the park early.

Adventureland combines the exotic islands of the Caribbean, Polynesia, and Southeast Asia. The landscaping features many plants and trees native to these islands. The buildings look like ones you might see if you traveled there. Adventureland has four main attractions. We were able to catch three of them—Pirates of the Caribbean, the Jungle Cruise, and the Swiss Family Treehouse. We didn't have time to see the Tropical Serenade, so it is described briefly at the end of the section.

Pirates of the Caribbean

See a pirate raid on a Caribbean island town as you float through this adventure. Cannons fire into the air while pirates attack and pillage a village. The song "Yo-Ho, Yo-Ho, A Pirate's Life For Me" is the ride's catchy theme. As you make your way through the different scenes, pay attention to details like the exploding flowerpots and the interesting faces of each pirate. Near the end, don't miss the pirate with his leg dangling over the bridge—the leg is actually hairy. There is one small flume drop during the ride, so be prepared.

"This is an excellent ride," says David. "My favorite part is the pirate ship with the wind blowing and all the cannons firing. I love how the characters look real," he adds.

Karyn thinks the details are great, too. "I was really paying attention to things like the hair on that guy's leg, the pirate chasing the lady, and the fire—it all just looks so real," she says. Ashley notices the characters, also. "The costumes are neat," she says.

But Lissy thinks the ride is a little

"It all just looks so real."
—Karyn (age 13)

it's still a cool ride," she says.

Robert agrees. "My favorite part has to be the drop," he says. "I thought the pirate was pointing his gun right at me—that was cool. The only part I wasn't crazy about was the skull and crossbones. It was too dark."

"My favorite part is the pirate ship with the wind blowing and all the cannons firing."
—David (age 13)

dull. "It's really slow and I'm not that into pirates, so it doesn't amuse me too much." Brian agrees. "It isn't as exciting as I thought it would be," he says. "I do like all the details and the way things look very realistic—especially the pirate's hairy leg."

Nita's favorite part is the dip: "There should be more dips, but

Jungle Cruise

Become an explorer on this journey through four far-away lands—a Southeast Asian jungle, the Nile valley, the African veldt, and an Amazon rain forest. Along the way you'll see elephants, zebras, giraffes, lions, hippos, and even headhunters. The captain of the ship tells lots of corny jokes, so how much you enjoy this ride will depend on your guide. This ride is usually very crowded. Ask if the wait is more than 15 minutes. If it is, come back at another time.

Some of the kids think the ride is a little dull. "There isn't enough action in it," says David. "It would be neat if you got wet."

Nita agrees. "I think it's boring and not a good ride for teenagers," she says. "I'd recommend it if you have nothing better to do on a hot day."

Karyn thinks the Jungle Cruise is a "nice family ride. But the guide has a lot to do with how much you like it, and our guide wasn't very good."

Ashley agrees. "I did not like our guide. His jokes were really stupid," she says.

Lissy and Robert like the Jungle Cruise. "The driver let me drive the boat for a while and that was really fun," says Lissy. "I like the way all the fake animals look real," she adds.

Robert agrees. "I love the ride," he says. "It would be even cooler if the headhunters really threw their spears."

Don't wait more than 15 minutes for this ride.

Swiss Family Treehouse

Before you go see the treehouse, it's a good idea to know something about the classic story of the Swiss Family Robinson. The Robinsons were traveling to America when their ship was wrecked on an island in a storm. Mr. Robinson and two of his three sons built a treehouse. Although the family was given several chances to leave the island, all but one son decided to stay. The treehouse was so comfortable that the family had "everything we need right at our fingertips," said Mr. Robinson.

Disney's version of the treehouse has many levels that you climb by way of a staircase. There are patchwork quilts on the beds, and there is running water in every room.

The tree is a creation of the Walt Disney World props department. It has 800,000 plastic and vinyl leaves. Its concrete roots are set 42 feet into the ground.

Everyone agrees that reading the story or seeing the Disney movie about the Swiss Family Robinson makes the treehouse much more fun to explore.

"You have to know the story to

Try to read the book or see the movie about the Swiss Family Robinson before you visit this attraction.

understand it," says Karyn. "It's so neat after you know what you're looking at. My favorite room is the kitchen," she adds.

"Once you know the story, then the treehouse is fascinating," says David. "I like the boys' room with the hammocks and the running water."

Lissy agrees. "You wouldn't know why they built the treehouse in the first place. They did a good job of disguising it because it looks like a real tree."

Ashley likes the treehouse and says "the kitchen is my favorite."

Robert has seen the movie and read the book, so he really understood what he was seeing. "I could name all the rooms as we walked around," he says. "It's an excellent treehouse."

What We Missed

Tropical Serenade was the very first Walt Disney World attraction with Audio-Animatronics figures. Your hosts are José, Michael, Pierre, and Fritz. They introduce you to more than 200 birds, flowers, and tiki statues who sing and whistle a variety of songs.

FRONTIERLAND

Frontierland represents the American Frontier—from New England to the Southwest—from the 1770s to the 1880s. It includes two of the most popular attractions in the park. Both are mountains. We took a watery trip down Splash Mountain, but Big Thunder Mountain Railroad was being renovated during our visit. Other attractions in Frontierland include the Country Bear Jamboree, the Diamond Horseshoe Jamboree, the Frontierland Shootin' Arcade, and Tom Sawyer Island.

Splash Mountain

This is the newest peak in the Disney mountain range—and the Magic Kingdom's newest thrill ride. At Splash Mountain, you travel in a log boat through brightly painted scenes from Walt Disney's movie, *Song of the South*. You'll see Brer Rabbit, Brer Fox, and Brer Bear getting into all kinds of trouble. There are three small dips

during the ride, all leading up to the big drop—a sharp plunge down 52 feet at a 45-degree angle going 40 miles per hour. If you're sitting in the front of the log, you get very wet. If you're in the back, you just get a small splash.

"It's really cool," says Taran. "The last drop is awesome."

HOT TIP:

Sit in the front of the log if you want to get wet.

Ashley agrees. "I like all the dips, but the last one is great. I like how my belly would flip-flop on the way down."

The kids agree that you have to go on the ride a few times before you can appreciate the scenery and the story about Brer Rabbit, Brer Bear, and Brer Fox. "The dips were incredible," says Brian. "But I didn't know what was going on inside the mountain."

Lissy agrees. "I didn't know the story, but when I heard the song "Zip-A-Dee-Doo-Dah" I knew where it was from. The big drop is awesome, but you don't get too wet if you're sitting in the back of the log."

Robert thinks "the scenery is really good, especially at the end when Brer Fox gets his tail pulled by an alligator. It's a very cool ride."

Karyn agrees. "All the characters are so cute and so detailed, and of course, the last drop is great."

"**The last drop is awesome!**"
—Taran (age 9)

Country Bear Jamboree

At this unusual country-and-western show, about 20 life-size Audio-Animatronics bears sing songs, play musical instruments, and tell a few jokes. It's a silly show, so it's important to go in with a silly attitude. Big Al, one of the most popular bears, can't even carry a tune.

The show got mixed reviews from the kids, with most of them not enthusiastic.

"It's strictly for little kids like ages 2 to 6," says Lissy. "It's a serious waste of time for older kids."

Karyn agrees, giving the show a rating of "two thumbs down and a

> ## "The bears are great, and some of them are very funny."
> —Brian (age 12)

couple of toes. But I think little kids will like to sing along with the characters," she adds.

"The show is very boring," says David. "I hate country music, so I really don't like this show."

Even though many of the kids don't like the show, some of them found something they thought was cute. For example, Ashley says she hates the show, "but the little bear that is unhappy and squeaks is kind of cute."

Brian, however, likes the show. "The bears are great, and some of them are very funny," he says. "The one that seems to be drunk and can't sing is really funny. I think the show is very enjoyable."

> ## "Two thumbs down and a couple of toes."
> —Karyn (age 13)

What We Missed

There are several other attractions in Frontierland. One major roller coaster—**Big Thunder Mountain Railroad**—was closed for renovation while we were there. Big Thunder has enough swoops and turns to keep it thrilling, but it's more tame than Space Mountain. The ride takes place inside and outside the huge mountain. The runaway mine trains pass through several scenes with some real-looking chickens, donkeys, possums, and goats. It's a ride that you can go on again and again, and still see new things each time.

Tom Sawyer Island, a small spot in the middle of the Rivers of

America, has hills to climb and a working windmill. There are two neat bridges. One is a swing bridge and the other is a barrel bridge. When one person bounces, everybody lurches and gets a good laugh. Across the bridges is Fort Sam Clemens, where there is a guardhouse with a bunch of Audio-Animatronics animals. The second floor of the fort has air guns that you can shoot.

Speaking of shooting, at the **Frontierland Shootin' Arcade**, you can fire rifles that send infrared beams at targets. Hit the tombstones and they rise, sink, and spin. Hit the gravedigger's shovel, and a skull pops out of the grave. (You have to pay extra to use the arcade. It's not included in your park admission.)

An energetic crew of singers and dancers perform all day at the **Diamond Horseshoe Jamboree**. The jokes are very corny, but the performers are entertaining.

LIBERTY SQUARE

Liberty Square is actually a small area that separates Frontierland from Fantasyland. It's a quiet spot with several shops and a couple of the Magic Kingdom's most popular attractions—the Haunted Mansion and the Hall of Presidents. We visited the Haunted Mansion but had to bypass the Hall of Presidents. Other Liberty Square attractions that we missed are the Liberty Square Riverboat and the Mike Fink Keel Boats.

Haunted Mansion

There are so many special effects inside the Haunted Mansion that you can go through it over and over again, and still not catch them all. It's not too scary, but there are enough surprises to keep you on your toes. When you enter the building, you are led into a hall where the host gives you an idea of what you're in for. The

"It's awesome! You never know what is going to come next."
—Lissy (age 11)

ceiling starts to rise and the walls begin to stretch—or at least that's how it seems. You're actually in an elevator that helps create these special effects. There is a moment before you board your "Doom Buggy" when the room is completely dark. It only lasts about 15 seconds, but for kids who are afraid of the dark, that's much too long.

Once on board your buggy, there are so many things to see. Try to watch for the raven that appears over and over again, the doorknockers that knock themselves, the ghostly teapot pouring tea, and the dancing ghosts.

"It's awesome," says Lissy. "It's kind of scary because you never know what is going to come next, so it's very surprising," she adds.

Ashley agrees. "I really like how you don't know what is going to happen next. But it would be cool if there were some real people popping out and scaring you."

Karyn likes the Haunted Mansion but warns that "if you scare easily, I wouldn't recommend it."

Robert thinks that's good advice. "It's fun at the start, but when the lady looks like she's being hung and then it gets pitch black, it's too scary," he says. "If you don't like the dark, this is not a ride for you."

David thinks younger kids would be frightened by the ride. "I would recommend it for older kids who understand there is no such thing as ghosts," he says. "The characters look real and some of the parts are pretty scary. But I like it," he adds.

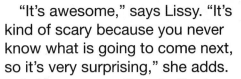

" If you don't like the dark, this is not a ride for you. "

—Robert (age 8)

What We Missed

The **Hall of Presidents** opens with a film that discusses the importance of the Constitution from the time it was written through the beginning of the Space Age. After the movie, you enter a theater where an Audio-Animatronics Abraham Lincoln reads off a roll call of all 42 American presidents, up through Bill Clinton. Each president responds with a nod.

The **Liberty Square Riverboat**, named *Richard F. Irvine* after a Disney designer, is a real steamboat. The ride is slow, but it's a nice break on a hot afternoon. The best seats are right up front or in the back, where you can see both sides of the Rivers of America as you go along.

Named for a riverboat captain who lived from 1770 to 1823 and traveled with Davy Crockett, the **Mike Fink Keel Boats** also take you on a ride along the Rivers of America.

PASTE
A
MAGIC
KINGDOM
PHOTO
HERE

MICKEY'S STARLAND

Even though this area is known as Mickey's Starland, the town itself is called Duckburg, U.S.A. Inside one of the large tents is the Mickey's Starland Show. The other big tent is the Mickey Mouse Club Funland, where an interactive video display lets you see yourself on a screen. There also are lots of hands-on activities. On the streets of Duckburg, you'll find Mickey's house. Be sure to notice some of the details there. Mickey's radio plays Disney songs, there are photos on the walls of Walt Disney and Mickey Mouse, and the television set shows the "Mickey Mouse Club."

Along the business street in Duckburg, you'll see the Popcorn Shop where boxes out front pop when they're opened. At the firehouse, there is a working siren and a rotating light. On the sidewalk, you'll see stars with the names of Disney characters in them. When you step on the star, you'll hear the character's voice.

At Grandma Duck's Farm, you can get up close to some baby animals. You can also see Minnie Moo, a cow with natural markings that look just like Mickey Mouse ears. Near the farm is the Mousekamaze, where trees and shrubs shaped like animals create a simple path for kids.

Mickey's Starland Show

This stage show stars Mickey Mouse and characters from the Disney Afternoon cartoons "Goof Troop," "Tale Spin," "Bonkers," and "Dark Wing Duck." Inside the pre-show area, you can watch clips from those cartoons and keep an eye on the countdown to showtime.

The show features a hostess who starts by singing a few songs with Mickey Mouse. Then she introduces the guest characters, like Goofy and his son Max, Bonkers, Baloo, Louie, and Dark Wing Duck. All the characters sing songs and act out skits, and the audience can sing along.

After the show, head for Mickey's dressing room, where you can get his autograph and have your photo taken with him.

"I love the songs they sing and how you can get up and dance."

—Nita (age 14)

The show gets mixed reviews from the kids.

"I just didn't like it," says Taran. "It's good for younger kids, but not for kids like 8 to 10."

Nita feels differently. "I love it," she says. "I love the songs they sing and how you can get up and dance." She thinks there is a middle age where kids don't appreciate the show, but then "when you get to be around my age, you like it again." She agrees that it's great for little kids, too.

Like Nita, Karyn loves the show, "but I think there's a certain age when you don't appreciate it."

Brian likes the show but says, "If I were a little younger, I would have liked it more. But I like watching the younger kids have fun," he adds.

David agrees. "Just seeing all the little kids have fun and enjoy the show is exciting and funny," he says.

"I like the show because I watch all those cartoons, especially "Goof Troop," says Robert. "I also think it's good because you can sing along if you want to, but you don't have to."

"I like the show because I watch all those cartoons."

—Robert (age 8)

FANTASYLAND

Many of Walt Disney World's kiddie rides are in Fantasyland, but there are a few attractions that older kids and even grown-ups will enjoy. We visited most of Fantasyland's rides during the 3 P.M. Main Street parade—and we suggest you do the same. These attractions are very popular, and the lines are much shorter while most people are at the parade. So it's a good idea to skip the parade on the day you tour Fantasyland, and use that time to go on the rides. Catch the parade on another day, when you'll be in other parts of the Magic Kingdom.

Cinderella's Golden Carrousel

Just about all of the attractions at Walt Disney World were designed and built by Imagineers. The carousel is one exception. It was built around 1917. Imagineers

Don't Forget

If the line is long, save the carousel for another time.

discovered it in New Jersey, where it was once part of an amusement park.

When you climb up on a horse for your ride on the carousel, be sure to notice that each one is different. And remember to look up at the ceiling and its hand-painted

"You can never grow too old for a carousel."

—Lissy (age 11)

scenes from *Cinderella*. While you ride, enjoy famous Disney tunes including "Zip-A-Dee-Doo-Dah," "When You Wish Upon A Star," and "Chim-Chim-Cheree."

"I think you can never grow too old for a carousel," says Lissy. "The horses are beautiful and the music makes it great," she adds.

Robert agrees. "I love the carousel and I love the music. I think people of any age would like it."

Some of the other kids feel differently. "It's very boring and babyish," says Ashley. David agrees. "I think it goes on forever and it's boring," he says.

Nita found a way to make the ride more fun for everyone by clapping in time with the music. "It's boring so that's why I started clapping," she says. Brian thinks that helps a lot. "I didn't like it until we all started clapping," he says. "Then it was kind of fun."

Karyn thinks the carousel is a nice, relaxing ride. "It's fun when we all were clapping, and it's nice to just rest for a little while."

All the kids agree that they wouldn't wait in a long line to ride.

Mad Tea Party

The idea for the oversize teacups that spin wildly through this ride was taken from a scene from *Alice In Wonderland*. In it, the Mad Hatter throws himself a tea party to celebrate his un-birthday. On the Mad Tea Party ride, you control how fast the cups spin by turning the big wheel in the center. The more you turn, the more you spin. Or you can just sit back and spin slowly with the movement of the ride. It may be difficult while you're spinning, but try to take a peek at the little mouse who keeps popping out of the big teapot in the center.

> **"You can go as fast or as slow as you want."**
>
> **—Brian (age 12)**

"It's a very good ride and it really makes you dizzy," says Nita. Brian agrees. "I wish it would go even faster, but it's good that you can go as fast or as slow as you want," he says.

Robert says, "The ride is really cool. I think they should have power steering, though."

David advises that the ride works best if everyone in the cup works together. "You have to coordinate," he says. "Sometimes you can go faster if fewer people work at spinning the wheel."

All the kids agree about two things: The ride is too short (it lasts about two minutes), and it would be better if there were a button to push instead of the wheel to spin. "Your arms get tired after a while," says Lissy, "but the teacups are always fun."

Dumbo, The Flying Elephant

Just like the star of the movie *Dumbo*, the elephants at this attraction fly. You can climb aboard and take a short ride (about two minutes) up and over Fantasyland. A button lets you control the up and down movement of the elephant. Timothy Mouse, who becomes Dumbo's manager in the movie, sits on top of a mirrored ball in the middle of the flying elephants.

The kids agree that this ride is more for younger children from ages three to eight. But they all think it would be fun to go on with a younger brother or sister.

"I think it's great for younger kids," says Karyn. "It's pretty boring for kids my age, though."

David says, "The fact that you could press a button and go higher I found interesting. But other than that, it's really boring."

Robert thinks "it's fun to go up really high. I think some little kids might be scared of the height, though."

Brian recommends it for younger children. "It's not a bad ride and I think little kids would love it," he says.

"**It's not a bad ride and I think little kids would love it.**"

—Brian (age 12)

Peter Pan's Flight

Swoop and soar through scenes that tell the story of how Wendy, Michael, and John get sprinkled with pixie dust, head for "the second star to the right and straight on till morning," and fly off to Never-Never-Land with Tinkerbell. Along the way they meet up with Princess Tiger Lilly, the evil Captain Hook, and his sidekick Mr. Smee. Near the end of the trip, there's a beautiful scene of London at night. Notice that the cars on the streets really move. Also, watch out for the crocodile who is about to eat Captain Hook for dinner.

When you first board the cars, which look like pirate ships, it seems like you're riding on a track on the ground. Once you get going the track is actually above you, so

you feel like you're really flying.

"I love this ride," says Robert. "I like how it makes you feel like you can fly. I especially like the part at the end with the crocodile."

Ashley agrees. "I like how you fly, and the city scene is neat with all the cars going up and down," she says. "I also like how it's so dark."

Lissy enjoys "how you fly over all the scenes from the story. I really like the music, too." Nita finds the ride "very relaxing. I think it really brings out the kid in you," she adds.

David points out that Peter Pan's Flight is different from all the other rides because "you're hooked from the top instead of being on a track below you." He adds, "I never get tired of this ride."

Brian likes all the details, like the costumes and colors of the characters. "I like how it shows parts from the movie *Peter Pan*," he says "and I like it that you're flying instead of riding on the ground."

"**It really brings out the kid in you.**"

—Nita (age 14)

It's A Small World

This is a boat ride through a mini wonderland. Boats take you slowly through several large rooms where beautiful, Audio Animatronic dolls represent different parts of the world. There are wooden soldiers, cancan dancers, Dutch children, Greek dancers, snake charmers, hot-air balloon fliers, leprechauns, bagpipers, and many more. There is even a jungle scene with hippos, giraffes, monkeys, and elephants.

All this colorful scenery is set to the song "It's A Small World," which plays over and over again. It's important to pay attention to all the details of the costumes on the dolls, and it's fun to try to guess which country the dolls are from. There are usually two lines at this attraction, and the one on the left is almost always shorter.

"I love all the costumes, the different dolls, and the customs," says Karyn. "It never gets old because of all the detail. Every time you go, you see something new," she adds.

Nita agrees that "the costumes are adorable, and I like the expressions on the dolls. But I don't like the ride. It's just too slow. If it had a few dips it would be better."

David also thinks the ride should go faster and have some dips. "I don't hate it, but I think it's better for younger kids. I'd enjoy taking

"Every time you go you see something new."

—Karyn (age 13)

my little brother on it," he says.

Lissy agrees that the ride is a little slow, but "it's really pretty and there are so many neat things to look at that it doesn't matter."

Ashley thinks the song gets a little tiring. "I really like how the costumes and cultures are, but the song just keeps going over and over. That I don't like."

Brian likes the scenery, but thinks the ride could be a little shorter. "The figures are neat, and I love all the colors and costumes. It should be shorter, though."

Pick the line on the left—it's almost always shorter.

Mr. Toad's Wild Ride

Mr. Toad is not a very good driver. So when you hop into one of his cars heading to "Nowhere in Particular," you're in for a wild trip. The cars go zigging and zagging around sharp turns. You crash through a fireplace, just miss being hit by a falling suit of armor, go through haystacks and barn doors into a chicken coop, and then ride down a railroad track on a collision course with a speeding train.

Most of the kids agree that Mr. Toad's Wild Ride is for younger kids, although there are a few scary moments that might frighten them.

"It's good for younger kids," says Karyn. "It's pretty boring for someone my age."

David agrees that it's a kiddie ride. "Some of the characters are funny, but it's really just for younger kids," he says. "I don't like that the characters are all made out of cardboard."

But Lissy thinks the scenery is "neat and I like how they have everything moving. When I saw the train coming, it was a little scary," she says. Robert agrees, "It sort of scared me a little bit."

Brian thinks the soundtrack is too loud. "The ride is good for younger kids, but the noise might scare them."

> **"Some of the characters are funny, but it's really just for younger kids."**
>
> —David (age 13)

Snow White's Adventures

As you travel along through this attraction, you see the scariest parts from the story of *Snow White and the Seven Dwarfs*. The Snow White character is never actually seen. That's because you are supposed to be Snow White. And you encounter all the problems she did with the evil witch, who keeps popping up. There also are a couple of scary skeletons. Near the end of the ride, the witch throws a boulder

"The witch hops out so close to you."
—Ashley (age 11)

toward each car. Then you see stars as if you were hit in the head with the rock.

There are lots of turns, and that witch seems to be around each one of them. During most of the ride it's very dark, so it can get pretty scary—especially for younger kids.

The kids agree that this attraction doesn't fit well into any age category. It's very scary for young children and a little boring for older kids.

"I think it's too scary for little kids," says Karyn. "If it's going to be a kiddie ride, there should be more happy parts in it." Lissy agrees. "There's nothing nice in the ride, just the scary stuff."

Ashley likes the ride, and says, "It's so funny. We were screaming and that made it more fun. But I think it would be too scary for young kids because the witch hops out so close to you."

Brian likes the fact that there are scenes during the ride that are like the movie, but he agrees, "Little kids would be terrified seeing the wicked witch."

What We Missed

Magic Journeys is a 3-D movie that follows a little boy through a variety of outdoor scenes. Some of the 3-D effects are great, especially when the boy blows on a dandelion and when the kite he is flying seems like it's heading straight for you.

The **Skyway** cable cars that run between Fantasyland and Tomorrowland offer a bird's-eye view of the Magic Kingdom. It's best to board the cars at Tomorrowland where the lines are shorter.

At **20,000 Leagues Under the Sea**, which we skipped because the lines were very long, Captain Nemo takes you on an undersea journey. The submarine is very realistic, but the underwater sights like the fish, shells, and plants look fake. Take a ride if the line is short, but don't bother waiting a long time.

TOMORROWLAND

Tomorrowland was designed as Walt Disney World's version of the future. But the present keeps catching up, so most of the land will be renovated soon to include some brand-new attractions. One thing is sure to stay the same—Space Mountain, which is the Magic Kingdom's most popular attraction. During our visit, we took two trips on this ride. We also went on the Grand Prix Raceway and Delta Dreamflight. The attractions we missed are described at the end of this section.

Space Mountain

Roller coaster fans will want to head straight for Space Mountain and its fast, winding trip through the galaxy. You'll travel in a rocket, in the dark (but not pitch black), with stars and meteors all around.

The kids agree that the turns and pretty steep dips of Space Mountain make for the best ride at the Magic Kingdom. On our last day there, we had time for one more ride. We gave the kids a choice of either Space Mountain or Splash Mountain. The vote was unanimous: Space Mountain.

Once you get inside the mountain, you choose between two lines. "I think sitting on the left side is better because there are more dips and more turns," says Karyn. Taran also prefers the left. "You get a little whiplash, but that's good," he says. "A big whiplash like you get on some roller coasters is too much."

Nita has a warning for kids who are not sure if they want to go on: "It goes too fast for somebody like me. I'm not a roller coaster person, and I felt like I was about to fall out when it went sideways." Another bit of good advice from Taran: "If you tend to get motion sickness, don't eat before you go on this ride."

The ride lasts just over 2½ minutes. "Waiting in line you think

Don't Forget

Never eat right before going on Space Mountain

'The ride is only two minutes long! That's not long enough,'" says Lissy. "Then you get on and two minutes seems too long," she says. Brian feels differently. "I was just getting into it and then it was over."

All the kids agree that the ride is "good scary." Anything "bad scary" happened only in their imaginations. David thinks that "the cranking noise sounds like the track is breaking." Lissy thinks "they should make it darker so you don't look down and see all the black tracks."

But don't worry: The roller coaster is perfectly safe to go on as many times as you want.

At the end of the ride, there is a moving walkway that leads you back outside the building. But first it takes you through RYCA 1/ Dream of a New World. This exhibit shows what electronic media might be like in the future. Toward the end of the walkway, you can see yourself on television monitors, so be sure to look up.

notes

Delta Dreamflight

Trace the history of aviation on a journey that takes you from man's first attempts at flight through the many advances in technology. The start of the trip features a giant pop-up book to show you that the story of flight is about to unfold. As you ride along, you'll see two movie sequences that make you feel like you're part of the action.

You'll also see a full-size section of the first type of commercial airplane to cross the Atlantic Ocean. A close look shows how luxurious travel was in those days. Other scenes depict life in foreign countries, where air travel made it possible for people to visit.

Near the end of the ride, you pass through a jet engine. Special effects and graphics re-create the engine's rotation and make you feel like you're spinning. The last scene is another pop-up book showing London and New York.

The kids think this ride needs a narrator. "An announcer to explain all the things you're seeing would be good," says Taran. "This is a learning ride, so they should teach more," he adds.

The kids gave high marks to the movie sequence that makes you feel like you're flying and to the spinning engine. "When you're watching the movie, it's like you're actually there," says Robert. "I like the big pop-up books, too."

Karyn thinks they should show

> "**When you're watching the movie, it's like you're actually there.**"
>
> —Robert (age 8)

some of the failures of flight as well as the successes. "I really like this ride, but I'm not sure other kids my age would," she says. "It may be too slow for teenagers."

Nita agrees. "It's boring to me except for the spinning engine," she says. "I'd recommend it more for older people."

Brian thinks the ride gets better as it goes along. "When it first starts, it goes so slow. But then it makes you feel like you are flying and going much faster than you really are. That's pretty neat."

Grand Prix Raceway

You can drive your own car (as long as you're 52 inches tall) on a lap around the racetrack at the Grand Prix. The cars travel along a track, but it's not as easy as it looks. Even expert drivers have some trouble. The cars are real and are powered by gasoline. They have rack-and-pinion steering and disc brakes and travel at about seven miles per hour.

"No matter how perfectly you drive, it always goes off the track," says Nita.

Brian agrees. "It feels like you don't have very good control of the car and you don't go very fast," he says.

Some of the kids really enjoy driving their own cars. "I love it. I thought it went pretty fast and I like having my own car," says Robert. Ashley agrees. "It's fun driving my own car. I think they should have it without the track."

David and Karyn think the ride gets boring once you've done it a few times. "I like the ride, but I wish they didn't have the track in the middle. It gets a little boring after a while," says David.

Karyn agrees. "It used to be one of my favorites, but it's a little boring now," she says. "I don't think very young kids would like it because they can't drive, and that's the whole fun of it."

"It's fun driving my own car."

—Ashley (age 11)

space probe.

For an overview of Tomorrowland, hop on the **WEDway PeopleMover**, which travels alongside or through most of the land's attractions. If you're not sure about going on Space Mountain, you can get a good view of the ride to help you decide. It's also interesting to note that the PeopleMover runs on a motor with no moving parts. It does not emit any pollution.

The **Carousel of Progress** shows how electricity has improved life in America. If you're dying to ride the **Skyway** cable cars that travel from Tomorrowland to Fantasyland and back, this is your best chance. The lines at the Tomorrowland station are much shorter, so board here.

Last but not least, **CircleVision 360: American Journeys** is a 360-degree movie with beautiful scenes of most of the United States, from New York to Alaska. There are sequences that make you feel like you are flying, and a look at the Mount St. Helens volcano just two days after it erupted. There's also a great scene of the launching of the Space Shuttle *Columbia*.

What We Missed

Star Jets tower above Tomorrowland and offer a quick, high-flying trip in rocketships. A lever lets you control your up-and-down movements. The lines are often long here, and since this ride is not very different from similar rides at many amusement parks, it's probably not worth a long wait.

The seats tilt and shake and oversize speakers let out loud hisses at **Mission To Mars**. The movie includes actual footage of Mars, taken by the Mariner Nine

AWESOME
(See at Least Twice)

WAY COOL
(Don't Miss)

My visit to The Magic Kingdom will include . . .

Space Mountain

Splash Mountain

Big Thunder
Mountain Railroad

The Haunted
Mansion

Peter Pan's Flight

Pirates of the
Caribbean

Grand Prix
Raceway

Mickey's
Starland

COOL
(Check it Out)

YAWN
(Save For Last)

It's A Small World

Jungle Cruise

Swiss Family Treehouse

Mad Tea Party

Mr. Toad's Wild Ride

Snow White's Adventures

Cinderella's Golden
Carrousel

Walt Disney World
Railroad

Country Bear Jamboree

Delta Dreamflight

Dumbo, The Flying Elephant

Epcot Center

Epcot, which stands for "Experimental Prototype Community of Tomorrow," is divided into two sections: Future World and World Showcase. The two worlds are separated by a very large lake known as World Showcase Lagoon.

When you first enter Epcot Center, you are in Future World. The pavilions here have exhibits and rides that explore communication, transportation, energy, imagination, the ocean, agriculture, and health. These topics may sound a little dull, but with just a few exceptions, the kids really enjoyed them.

World Showcase is a group of countries—Canada, the United Kingdom, France, Morocco, Japan, the United States, Italy, Germany, China, Norway, and Mexico—all arranged around the lagoon. Each country has distinctive landmarks that look just like the ones they are modeled after.

There are a few movies to see, plus a ride through Norway and Mexico. But mostly, World Showcase is designed to give you the flavor of the different cultures. The people who work at the pavilions and in the restaurants and shops are actually from the represented countries.

FUTURE WORLD

SPACESHIP EARTH

The symbol of Epcot Center is the giant silver ball that you can see from almost anywhere in the park. Inside the ball is the Spaceship Earth Show, a ride through the history of communications. You travel in a "time machine" from the days of Cro-Magnon man (30,000 to 40,000 years ago) to the present. The highlight of the trip comes when your time machine reaches the top of the dome and you can see thousands of tiny stars.

The older kids like this attraction more than the younger ones. "I think it's boring," says Robert. "I just about fell asleep."

Ashley remembers that she didn't like the ride when she was younger, but "now it's much more interesting to me," she says.

"The idea of being inside the ball

is cool," says Karyn. "Knowing that during the whole ride you're actually inside the huge thing you see outside is amazing," she adds.

"I love it," says Nita. "The details are great, like the monk who is snoring. I especially love the Greek scene."

Noticing the details makes the ride much more interesting. Be sure to observe that the hieroglyphics in the Egyptian scene are real. Notice, in the scene with the printing press, that the keys really work. Also, look at Michelangelo painting the ceiling of the Sistine Chapel and how his arm moves back and forth.

"It's a relaxing, informative ride," says Brian. "I like how you could see all the different times of history and how people communicated."

David agrees. "You see the entire history of the communications revolution," he says. "I especially like the end, when you see all the stars. It's really neat to realize you're at the top of the ball."

All the kids say they would like to see the show updated to include video phones, cellular phones, and other communications breakthroughs.

Don't go to Spaceship Earth first thing in the morning because that's when it's most crowded.

THE LIVING SEAS

Explore the deep waters of the Caribbean Sea in the world's largest aquarium. There are more than 5,000 sea creatures, including sharks, dolphins, barracuda, angelfish, sea lions, and many more. Your sea exploration begins in the waiting area, where there are samples of old wet suits worn by the first divers. Then you see a video presentation and a movie. Next, you get on board a "hydrolator" to go down to explore the coral reef. Ask your parents if the hydrolator takes them deep underground. Then tell them they've actually traveled less than an inch.

After a ride through the aquarium, you are left off at Sea Base Alpha. This is your chance to take a closer look at the creatures of the sea and to try out the many hands-on exhibits.

"Living Seas is really cool," says Robert. "I thought my ears popped in the hydrolator. It feels like you're going way down to the bottom of

> "It feels like you're going way down to the bottom of the sea."
> —Robert (age 8)

she says, "but I prefer to see the real animals."

Taran and Robert agree. "The manatees are really cool," Taran says. And Robert adds, "I saw a spotted eagle ray, which is like a stingray. That was cool, too."

the sea, even though you're only going down three-quarters of an inch," he adds.

David says, "It's fun learning about the different kinds of fish in the oceans."

Brian likes the hands-on exhibits. "You can put your arms in a diving suit and try to move like you're in the ocean," he says.

Nita and Taran tried the diving suit test together. "We didn't pass," Nita says. "It's really difficult to do things in a suit like that. It shows how hard it is for real divers." Taran explains, "I reached out and pulled the lever, but nothing happened. It's really hard."

Karyn "just loves the manatees. The rest of the exhibits are okay,"

THE LAND

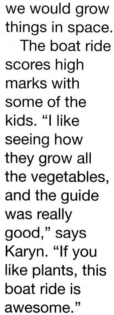

This pavilion focuses on one of everybody's favorite subjects—food. There is a boat ride through a greenhouse and a funny show about food, plus a movie about the environment and special guided tours.

Listen to the Land Boat Ride

Set out on a journey that takes you through a simulated rain forest, a desert, and a prairie. See experimental technology that's used to grow plants in different environments. There's a desert farm with a drip irrigation system and an area where lettuce is grown in zero gravity to demonstrate how we would grow things in space.

The boat ride scores high marks with some of the kids. "I like seeing how they grow all the vegetables, and the guide was really good," says Karyn. "If you like plants, this boat ride is awesome."

" It shows how plants can grow in desert sand. "
—Brian (age 12)

Brian says, "I like the ride because it shows how plants can grow in soils like desert sand, which is very difficult."

Robert and Ashley feel differently. "People who like plants would like it, but I don't," says Robert. Ashley says, "I'm not into plants so I thought it was a little boring. But I did like seeing some of the little vegetables like the cucumbers."

Kitchen Kabaret Revue

Bonnie Appetit is the star of this show presented by characters who sing about healthy eating. The Kitchen Krackpots band provides the tunes for acts by Mr. Dairy Goods, the Boogie Woogie Bak'ry Boy, the Cereal Sisters, the Fiesta Fruit, Mr. Hamm and Mr. Eggz, and many other cute characters. There are songs, jokes, and some special effects that make the show entertaining.

"It's really cute and I like the costumes," says Ashley. Nita agrees. "I think it's cute, too. And I learned about the food groups and what they consist of," she adds.

Karyn "would recommend the show for little kids." So would David. "I think they would like all the characters," he says.

Look for some of the details that make this show fun, but often go over kids' heads. For instance, Ashley noticed, "There was smoke coming out of the pan with the ham and eggs, and when the dairy lady was singing I saw that the radio station call letters on her microphone are KOW."

There are two other attractions at The Land Pavilion that we did not get to see. **Symbiosis** is a movie that examines the balance between technology and the environment. It includes stories about pollution and scenes about rivers that have been rescued from ruin.

For kids (and parents) who are very interested in plants and the environment, there is the **Harvest Tour**, a more detailed, 45-minute guided look at the topics covered on the boat ride.

JOURNEY INTO IMAGINATION

Your host for this pavilion is Figment—a magical creature created from a lizard's body, a crocodile's nose, a steer's horns, two big yellow eyes, two small wings, and a pinch of childish delight. Figment is most often thought of as a baby dragon. He is so popular that he has become a mascot for Epcot Center.

Inside the pavilion is a ride through the wonders of the imagination, a hands-on activity center called Image Works, and a

> " They have everything
> a kid could need
> to occupy himself. "
> —Lissy (age 11)

3-D movie called *Captain EO* that stars Michael Jackson. Outside the pavilion are the Serpentine Fountains, whose streams of water arc from one garden to another in the most amazing way.

Time was running short for us so we decided to skip the ride and the movie and spend our visit at Image Works.

Image Works

Once you get inside Image Works, it may be hard to leave. This is heaven for kids, with lots of hands-on (and feet-on) activities. The Rainbow Corridor is a tunnel full of neon tubes in all the colors of the rainbow. Walk through it and you'll reach Stepping Tones, where you step on colored lights on the floor to trigger different sounds. It's especially fun when you're with lots of people and everyone joins in. Other activities include Lumia, a seven-foot plastic ball that shows swirling lights and colors when different voices are heard. The Magic Palette has a special stylus and a touch-sensitive screen that let you create all kinds of images using day-glo colors. At the Electronic Philharmonic you can conduct an orchestra by raising and lowering your hands.

"This place is totally awesome," says Lissy. "They have everything a kid could need to occupy himself."

Nita agrees. "There's so much to do. My favorite was directing the band." Ashley thinks "the lights and colors are really cool, and it's neat how many things there are to do."

David likes "having all the hands-on experiences. It's a very fun place," he says.

Serpentine Fountains

The arcing streams of water move from one garden plot to the next with no obvious pattern. That makes this area a highlight with kids of all ages.

"If you stand in the right place you can get totally wet," says Taran. "It's one of my favorite things." Robert agrees. "It's really cool and I like getting wet," he says.

Nita thinks it's neat "how the water jumps over your head." And Lissy likes the fountains because "they keep you on your toes. If you're hot, you can just stand there and get a refreshing break," she says.

"**If you stand in the right place you can get totally wet.**"

—Taran (age 9)

The **Journey Into Imagination Ride** takes you on a tour of the imagination and how it works. Figment and his pal Dreamfinder lead the way to show how the five senses send messages to the brain. About three-quarters of the way through the ride, you'll see a flash of light. Be sure to smile because your picture is being taken.

Captain EO, a 3-D movie starring Michael Jackson, finds the pop star trying to transform a dismal planet into a happy place through the magic of music and dance. There are many 3-D special effects, and Jackson performs several songs written just for this movie.

Sketch Pad

HORIZONS

Get a taste of life in the future as you make your way through scenes showing a typical family in different environments. In the first scene, transportation and communication systems—such as holographic telephones and magnetic-levitation trains—help keep faraway family members close. The second scene shows robots harvesting fruits and vegetables that have been grown in a desert. The third scene takes place in a floating city, where schoolchildren take underwater field trips. The last setting is in space, where family members stay in shape by playing games like zero-gravity basketball.

What happens at the end of the ride is up to you and the three other people in your car. Majority rules as you choose from land, sea, or space. Your car tilts back and vibrates, and special sound effects and close-up film sequences make you feel like you're moving very fast.

"I like the part where you choose where you want to go," says Nita.

> "They show you how they think the future will be."
> —Ashley (age 11)

You can choose your own ending, but majority rules in each car.

everyone was eating. I like that they show you how they think the future will be."

Robert agrees. "It's a cool ride because it shows how the future might be," he says. He also likes that the cars turn sideways "so you can really see everything."

David thinks there's a lot to see along the way. "There are many details, like the scuba class going by in the beginning, which you see again later on," he says. "I like learning about everyone's hopes for the future."

"It should be longer, though, because it's very interesting."

Ashley says, "All the space outfits are neat, and in the underwater part it's cool how

WORLD OF MOTION

This is a humorous journey through the history of transportation. It begins with a caveman blowing on his red feet and winds up in a showroom of cars of the future. During the ride, you see how man invented the wheel and experimented with many types of transportation, including flying machines, balloons, steam trains, riverboats, stagecoaches,

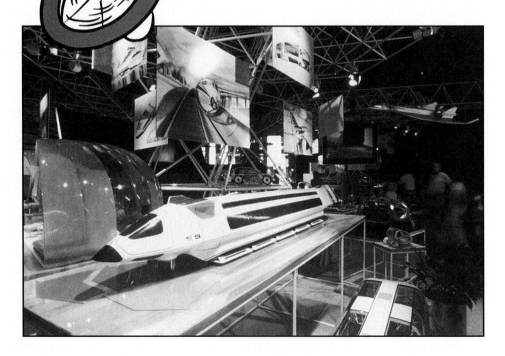

" **The speed rooms make you feel like you're flying.** "

—Brian (age 12)

airplanes, cars, and others. At the end of the history lesson, you ride through "speed rooms" that make you feel like you're going very fast. You end up in the Transcenter, where there are hands-on activities and prototype cars for the future.

"As the ride goes on, you learn about the history of transportation and how it evolved," says David. "I like cars, so this ride interests me a lot."

Robert loves this ride, "especially all the funny things, like the caveman blowing on his feet. And I really like the cars at the end," he adds.

Brian and Nita like the special effects. "The speed rooms make you feel like you're flying," says Brian. Nita agrees. "My favorite part is the speed rooms. I also like the cars at the end. I picked one out for myself!"

Ashley says, "I like the part where the cars are lined up with the families in them near the end. I like looking at all the futuristic cars, too."

Other exhibits at the Transcenter show some of the tests that cars must pass at the factory. Locks are tested, doors are opened and shut over and over again, keys are turned back and forth, and windows are put up and down without a break. There also is a short, animated film and some computers for hands-on fun.

" **I like the cars at the end. I picked one out for myself!** "

—Nita (age 14)

WONDERS OF LIFE

The newest pavilion at Future World has the kids' two favorite Epcot Center attractions— Body Wars, the rough ride through the human body, and Cranium Command, a great show about how the brain works. Also inside the building are many hands-on activities, *The Making of Me* (a movie about the birth of a baby), a cartoon show about health that stars Goofy, a stage show about anatomy, and much, much more. It's easy to spend a couple of hours here, so come early to beat the crowds.

Body Wars

Fasten your seatbelt for a very rough and bumpy ride through the human body. Before entering the vehicles, you are miniaturized for a special rescue mission to help a scientist who gets stuck while trying to remove a splinter. The ride takes place on a flight simulator, which is the same type of device used to train astronauts and pilots. Together, the simulator and the movie on the screen make you feel like you're really inside the body.

"For the roughest ride, try to sit in the back."
—Nita (age 14)

"You really have to hold on to the arms of the seats or you get thrashed around," warns Taran. "I think it should take longer to get from the heart to the brain, or that you should go all the way down to the feet and then bounce up to the brain," he adds.

Don't worry if some people in your group don't want to go on Body Wars. There are plenty of things for them to do at Wonders of Life. And you can meet them when you get off the ride.

The same technology is used at Star Tours at the Disney-MGM Studios Theme Park, but Body Wars is a much rougher ride.

"It's a little too bumpy for me," says Karyn. "I do like all the special effects but it's too jerky." Brian feels the same way. "You really get jerked around too much, and I don't like that kind of ride," he says.

The ride is still a favorite for most of the kids. "I love it," says Robert. "It's not scary at all, and it's cool and fun the way you go through the body." Ashley agrees. "I really like bumpy rides, so I like this one a lot."

Nita has been on it a few times "and I still like it. For the roughest ride, try to sit in the back," she advises.

Cranium Command

Imagine that you're a pilot. But instead of flying an airplane, you pilot the brain of a 12-year-old boy. That's what happens to Buzzy in this attraction. The first part of the show takes place outside the theater, in a preview area. There you see a funny movie that explains how Buzzy gets his job. Then you go into the theater—and inside the brain with Buzzy. You watch as he tries to get all the parts of the brain to work together.

"You think it will be a little story about the brain or something," says Taran. "Instead it turns out to be a really cool thing."

Lissy agrees. "I like it a lot

because you learn different things about the brain and how it works with the rest of your body—and you have a lot of fun at the same time." And Karyn thinks that "it is

60

HOT TIP:

Be sure to pay attention to the pre-show.

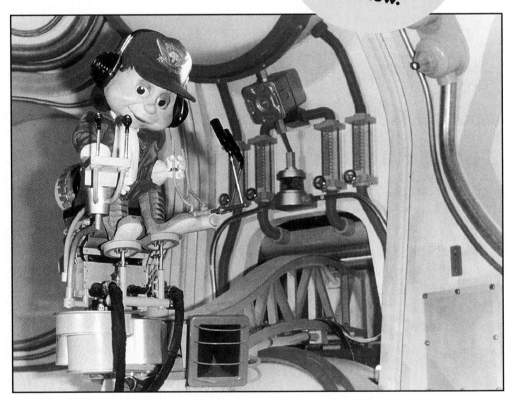

very educational as well as cute and funny."

Be sure to pay attention to that first movie because it explains what you will see in the theater. "If you didn't see the pre-show, you'd go crazy trying to figure out what was going on," Robert says. "And it was really funny, too."

The brain in Cranium Command belongs to a boy named Bobby. Once inside the brain, you see

Buzzy trying to pilot Bobby through a day at school. Nita likes "the part where his heart starts beating faster because he sees a pretty girl." Ashley likes how the parts of the brain were each played by a different character. She notices that "the left brain was the smartest, but the right just wanted to take the girl to a desert island." Robert adds that "the left brain is totally logical and the right brain is crazy."

The show taught David "not to be too stressed in bad situations." And it helped all the kids understand how the brain works. Besides, as Brian points out, "It was a lot of fun to see all the different things that go on in our brain each day."

The kids agree that Cranium Command is one attraction that is kind of hidden in the Wonders of Life Pavilion. None of them had ever seen it—even though some had been to the World before. So be on the lookout and don't miss it!

There are many other activities at the Wonders of Life Pavilion. **Goofy About Health** is a cartoon show about how Goofy goes from being a sloppy-living guy to a health-conscious fellow. At the **Anacomical Players Theater**, you see a corny but informative show about good health. **The Making of Me** is a movie about the birth of a baby with real scenes from a hospital.

There also are many hands-on activities. **Wonder Cycles** are computerized bicycles that allow you to watch film footage while riding. In the **Coach's Corner**, tennis, baseball, and golf swings are analyzed and you get tips for a better game. The **Sensory Fun House** has many different hands-on options. The kids enjoy trying to guess what certain objects are without being able to see them.

At the **Met Lifestyle Revue**, you can punch your age, weight, height, and other information into a computer, and it will tell you how to lead a healthier life.

The only serious part of the Wonders of Life Pavilion is **Frontiers of Medicine**. It features scientific and educational exhibits.

UNIVERSE OF ENERGY

This pavilion takes a look at the many ways in which energy was originally created—and how it's created today. It includes two films, an animated movie, and a ride through prehistoric times complete with huge dinosaurs. When you first enter the pavilion, you see a film about the types of energy in use today. Then an animated movie shows you what prehistoric Earth looked like and how fossil fuels were created.

The theater seats break up into several sections and take you into the prehistoric world of the animated movie. You travel through lots of fog, past huge trees, real-looking lava, and several types of dinosaurs

"The best part of the ride is when it's over."

—Robert (age 8)

including a
brontosaurus,
an allosaurus,
an elasmosaurus,
and pteranodons.
These are some of
the largest animals
of their type ever to
be made.

The vehicles then
move into another
theater, where you
see a movie about the
future of energy
exploration. This
movie lasts 12½
minutes—and seems
even longer. That's one
reason this attraction is
not a favorite with the
kids. "It's boring," says
Nita. "The dinosaurs are
okay, but the last movie is
way too long." Ashley
agrees. "I think the whole
thing is very boring," she
says.

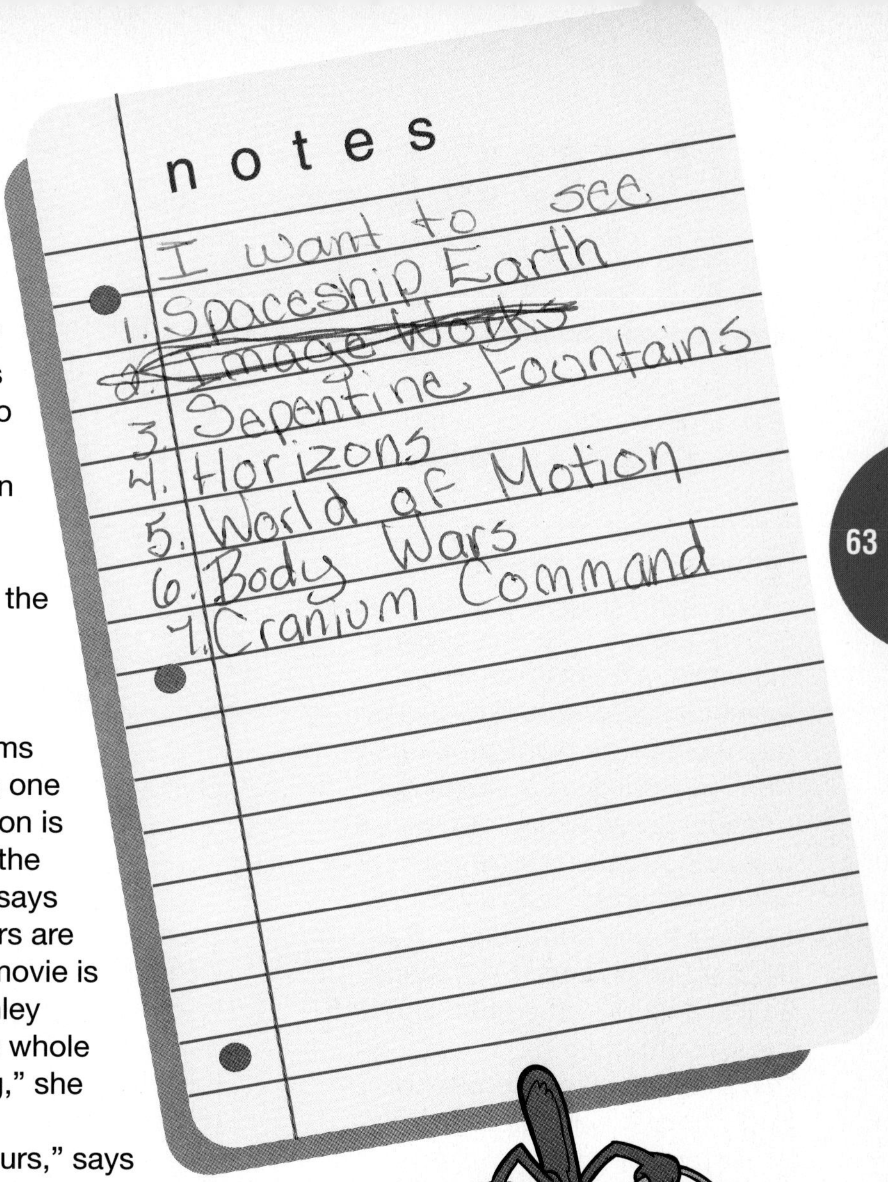

"I like the dinosaurs," says
David. "But the movies are so
boring that I grew restless. I
couldn't get enough good
information to make it enjoyable
for me."

Karyn feels the same way. "It's
very, very boring," she says. "I
think I slept for part of it." And
Robert thinks the "best part of the
ride is when it's over."

notes

I want to see
1. Spaceship Earth
2. Image Works
3. Serpentine Fountains
4. Horizons
5. World of Motion
6. Body Wars
7. Cranium Command

WORLD SHOWCASE

CANADA

The beauty of America's northern neighbor is on display at this pavilion. There is a rocky mountain, a rushing stream, beautiful gardens, and even a totem pole. The highlight at the Canada Pavilion is a movie, *O Canada!* It was filmed using a technology called CircleVision 360, so the Canadian scenery surrounds you completely. The theater has no seats. You stand, so it's easy to turn around and see the whole picture.

The movie takes a coast-to-coast look at Canada, including scenes of skiers, dogsledders, and ice skaters in the snowy Canadian Rockies. Eagles, bobcats, wolves, bears, deer, bison, and herds of reindeer were all filmed in their natural settings. Cities and towns are part of the film, too. You can also see covered bridges, sailing ships, and even the Royal Canadian Mounted Police.

"The movie is pretty and there are many beautiful scenes," says Nita. "But I don't like standing up. They need seats in that theater!"

Robert agrees. "I don't like having to stand," he says, "but the movie is okay."

> "**I like all the information the movie gives you about Canada.**"
>
> —Ashley (age 11)

Ashley likes how much she learned about Canada. "I like the music and I like all the information the movie gives you about Canada," she says. "The winter scenes are my favorites."

Karyn agrees. "All the mountains and sledding scenes are beautiful."

The CircleVision technique makes you feel like you're actually part of the movie. David explains, "I think it's neat how CircleVision makes you feel like you're moving. Plus the movie shows a lot of the culture of Canada, and I like seeing all the different buildings and the rivers."

Brian agrees. "I like how they make you feel like you're moving," he says. "I think it's great—I like every part of the film."

Lissy thinks the movie has a few boring spots, but "they explain Canada well. There should be more moving sensations, though."

Don't go to this movie if you're very tired. You have to stand for the whole film.

FRANCE

The Eiffel Tower is the most recognizable landmark at the France Pavilion. But it's not as tall as it seems. The same technique that makes Cinderella Castle appear taller than it is—forced perspective—is used here to make the Eiffel Tower seem to loom over Paris. The buildings are designed to look just like those you would see in a French town. The people who work at the pavilion all are French and speak English with a French accent.

The main attraction at the France Pavilion—aside from the delicious treats at the bakery—is *Impressions de France* (Impressions of France), an

18-minute movie that takes you from one end of France to the other. The movie is shown on a 200-degree screen, so you get to sit down and take in all the beautiful views. There are village scenes with flower markets, pastry shops, and lovely homes. There are shots of the real Eiffel Tower, the Palace of Versailles, the French countryside, wine and champagne vineyards, the Alps, the French Riviera, and much more. Even though it's not a CircleVision 360 movie, it really feels as if you're moving—especially in the skiing in the Alps scene. The music is the perfect soundtrack for the movie. Most of it is by French composers.

"This movie makes me want to go to France," says Taran, "especially for the skiing."

Karyn has been to France, and she recognized many of the places. "It's very interesting to me because I've been to a lot of parts of France. I think it's more fun if you know what you're looking at."

Nita and Ashley are less enthusiastic. "It just wasn't interesting to me," Nita says. Ashley agrees. "It doesn't give enough information about France."

> "This movie makes me want to go to France."
> —Taran (age 9)

But Lissy thinks the "pictures describe themselves. I'm not into studying different countries, but I like when you feel like you're moving," she says.

Robert says, "This is my favorite of the movies we saw at Epcot Center. I like that you can sit down and rest your legs."

Brian thinks the "music is great, and I like the skiing and what they show of the country."

CHINA

At the center of this pavilion is the Disney version of the Temple of Heaven, a landmark in the Chinese city of Beijing. Entertainers show off traditional Chinese dances with masks and streamers and music that adds to the overall atmosphere.

Inside the Temple of Heaven is another CircleVision 360 movie called *Wonders of China: Land of Beauty, Land of Time*. Before going in to see the movie, take a look at the waiting area. It's decorated in red and gold, and features exhibits on Chinese art and culture. When we were there, the exhibit was all about dragons.

Wonders of China is a stand-up movie like *O Canada!* The 19-minute film shows a view of China that most people—kids and grown-ups—have never seen. The Chinese cities and countryside, its people and all their ancient traditions are depicted. It is a beautiful movie, but one that is appreciated more by adults and by kids who have studied China.

"I think it's pretty interesting but that's because I just finished studying China a few weeks ago in school," says Nita.

Karyn prefers the waiting area. "The exhibit is cool and the marble benches are pretty," she says. "I think the movie is boring. I'm not really that interested in China," she adds.

Robert, who

> **"The dragon stuff is really cool."**
> —Robert (age 8)

"It's a complete yawn."

—David (age 13)

knows a lot about dragons, likes the waiting area. "The dragon stuff is really cool. They have some neat things in there, and since I love dragons, this was my favorite part," he says. "I think the movie is boring."

Most of the kids agree that the movie is better for their parents and other adults. "It's really boring—a complete yawn," says David. Lissy agrees. "I just don't think it's very interesting," she says.

NORWAY

The history, folklore, and culture of one of the world's oldest countries are the focus of this pavilion. The central building is a Norwegian castle, modeled after an ancient fortress that still stands in the capital city of Oslo. Inside is the Maelstrom ride through Norwegian history. You board dragon-headed Viking boats, the same type that Eric the Red sailed in.

The ride begins in a Viking village, where a ship is being built to go out to sea. The next scene takes place in the forest, where a three-headed troll curses the boat and causes it to start backing up. You are heading for a waterfall and the boat seems as if it will go over backwards. Then, just in time, it moves forward again. The ride has a few more unexpected dips and turns, and there are lightning flashes and other special effects.

After leaving the boats, you can see a movie about Norway that helps explain some of the history and folklore you see on the boat ride.

"I like how they make you think you're going down the waterfall backwards," says Brian. "I really believed it."

Robert agrees. "I love this ride. I wish we really could have gone down the waterfall backwards," he says.

The kids agree that the scenery is confusing if you don't know

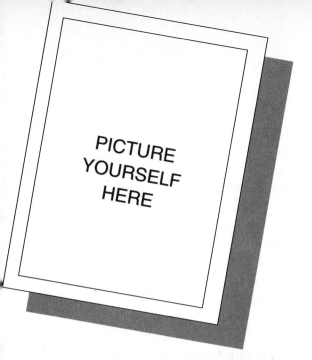

PICTURE
YOURSELF
HERE

much about Norway. "I think the movie should be first so you'll know what you're looking at," says Karyn. But Nita thinks "any ride with a dip is great."

David wishes the ride was longer. "But I still think it's the best thing in World Showcase, even though it's short." Ashley agrees. "It's too short and it should have some more dips," she says.

"I like how they make you think you're going down the waterfall."
—Brian (age 12)

WHAT WE MISSED

It would have taken two more days at Epcot Center to see everything. In World Showcase, the American Adventure Pavilion was closed for renovation so we missed the show there. We didn't have time to take in the boat ride at Mexico. The other pavilions—Morocco, the United Kingdom, Japan, Italy, and Germany—don't have attractions like rides or movies, but are fun to explore to learn more about the particular country.

UNITED KINGDOM

From London to the English countryside, the buildings at this pavilion give a varied view of the United Kingdom. Some details worth looking for include the smoke stains painted on the chimneys to make them look old and the thatched roofs that are really made of plastic broom bristles. A group of comedians often performs along World Showcase Promenade near this pavilion.

MOROCCO

Nine tons of handmade tile were shipped to Epcot Center to build the Moroccan Pavilion. Moroccan artists were also brought in to make sure the mosaics or tilework would be authentic. There are replicas of monuments from several cities, including Marrakesh and Fez. A working waterwheel takes care of the irrigation of the gardens around the pavilion.

JAPAN

The pagoda out front makes the Japanese Pavilion easy to spot. It's modeled after a pagoda in the city of Nara. The landscaping was done according to the strict Japanese method of garden design. Some of the trees that are found in a traditional Japanese garden will not survive in Orlando, so similar trees were used as substitutes. There are often musicians, dancers, and costumed entertainers performing on the promenade outside the pavilion.

THE AMERICAN ADVENTURE

This pavilion is the centerpiece of World Showcase. The building was constructed with 110,000 bricks that were each made by hand. The American Adventure Show inside celebrates the American spirit from the earliest days right up to the present. The show is narrated by Audio-Animatronics figures of Benjamin Franklin and Mark Twain. These two figures were made very recently, with the latest technology, so it's hard to tell they aren't real. From the Pilgrims landing at Plymouth Rock to Alexander Graham Bell to Charles Lindbergh to Jackie Robinson to Walt Disney, the show pays tribute to many of the heroes of our

GERMANY

There isn't a village in Germany quite like the one at Epcot Center. Instead, it's a combination of cities and small towns from all around the country. They are blended together to offer a German flavor. Try to stop by for a visit at the top of any hour so you can see and hear the specially designed glockenspiel chime.

MEXICO

The pyramid-shaped building at the Mexican pavilion is home to El Rio del Tiempo: The River of Time. This is a boat trip through scenes of Mexican life. It's much slower than the one at Norway, and David had seen it before. "You'll fall asleep—I guarantee it," he says. Outside the building, a mariachi band often plays popular Mexican songs.

country. Historic events are shown on large screens behind the characters. The show was just updated to include events that took place during the 10 years since Epcot Center opened.

ITALY

Venice, the Italian city known for its canals, is the inspiration for this pavilion. The tower is a smaller version of the Campanile in Venice. The main building was designed to look just like the Doges Palace. Be sure to notice the gondolas tied to the moorings in World Showcase Lagoon.

AWESOME
(See at Least Twice)

Body Wars

Cranium Comand

Image Works

Serpentine
Fountains

WAY COOL
(Don't Miss)

The
Living Seas

Horizons

Norway

The Land

My visit to Epcot Center will include . . .

France
Norway
United Kingdom
Moracco
Japan
The American Adveture
Mexico

COOL
(Check it Out)

Canada
(ages 12 and up)

France
(ages 12 and up)

Spaceship Earth

World of Motion

YAWN
(Save For Last)

China

Universe of Energy

Disney-MGM Studios Theme Park

The Disney-MGM Studios Theme Park lets you see some of the magic of making movies and television programs. There are attractions that take you behind the scenes to see how animated movies are made, how sound effects are created and edited into movies, how special effects are done, and how stunts are performed.

There also is a great 3-D movie starring the Muppets, a rough ride through space on a flight simulator, a show where you can star in some famous television scenes, a chance to get autographs from the Teenage Mutant Ninja Turtles, and a playground made from the *Honey, I Shrunk the Kids* movie set.

One of the best things about the Studios is that you can participate in a number of attractions. It's fun to be right in the action, so be sure to volunteer.

It's also interesting to realize that movies and television shows are actually filmed here. During your visit, you may get a peek at people working on the next Disney animated movie or an episode of the "Mickey Mouse Club" show. Remember to pick up an entertainment schedule so you can plan your tour around the park without wasting any time.

Indiana Jones Stunt Spectacular

Fire, explosions, daring escapes, and other special effects are demonstrated at this highly rated attraction. Stunt men and women perform scenes from the movie *Raiders of the Lost Ark* and show how special effects are created. The audience watches from a large amphitheater, and several members are chosen (though no children are allowed) to perform with the pros.

"I love this show. I think it's great for all ages," says Karyn. Ashley agrees, "I think it's really neat how they do all the special effects, and how the fire blows up and how the tumblers tumble off the roofs."

One of the best parts of the

show, according to all the kids, is the scene where the giant ball rolls down and seems to crush Indiana Jones. "I was at the edge of my seat!" says Brian. Robert was amazed at the size of the ball. "The ball seems really heavy, so it would be so hard to get run over and stay alive," he says.

The kids also love the stunt men and women, and how they show us that dangerous movie stunts can be performed safely. "I love how they were falling from the towers, and then they were always okay—it's really neat," says Brian.

Lissy says the music adds to the suspense and "the stunt people are just fantastic." Brian views it as pure excitement, "especially when three of them were jumping off the trampoline and one landed in a really neat roll."

Not just entertaining, this is a show where you can learn a lot about movie stunts. "They really explain everything they're doing, making it even more fun to watch," says Karyn. David was on his feet the whole time. "It's fascinating seeing how they can get away with tricks like that," he says, "like how the guy went underground when we thought he was being chomped up by the fan."

Nita sums it up this way: "It's a show you can see many times and never get tired of."

> **"I was at the edge of my seat!"**
> —Brian (age 12)

75

Star Tours

Soar into space on board an out-of-control StarSpeeder from the movie *Star Wars*. Each flight is piloted by a new recruit, Rex, who can't seem to find his way through giant ice crystals and other spaceships.

The ride takes place on a flight simulator, the same type of device used to train astronauts and pilots. The combination of the simulator and the movie on the screen makes you feel like you're really rocketing through space.

"It is really neat. It's funny when the pilot can't find the brakes," says Robert. "If you know what the movie *Star Wars* is like, you'll really like this ride."

Brian agrees. "I loved it. I didn't think it was scary at all—I just wished it would be longer. It really makes you feel like you're in space."

Try to go to Star Tours first thing in the morning, but not right after breakfast.

For Lissy, "it was my first time and I thought it was really cool. I like how the seats seem to move and how the screen looks so real."

Some of the kids had been on Star Tours several times before. For them, this time wasn't as much fun. "After you go on it about 10 times, it gets a little boring and seems short. But if you've never done it, it's a must," according to David. Ashley was on Star Tours for the second time and she says, "It wasn't as fun as the first, but I still liked it and I laughed at some of the funny stuff. It's fun to get bumped around."

An experienced rider who's been on Star Tours about 15 times, Nita offers this advice: "If you're a person who likes a really rough ride, try to sit in the back."

Karyn thinks she's been on it too many times, but still thinks "it's one of the best rides at Walt Disney World."

The Great Movie Ride

Take a ride through some of the most famous movies of all time. You pass through the sets from films including *Singin' in the Rain*, *The Wizard of Oz*, *Alien*, *Casablanca*, and *Mary Poppins*. You get caught in the middle of a shootout and come close to getting slimed by the Alien. The ride ends with a movie that shows clips from great films.

"It was really cool, but it could have more action in it," says Robert. But Brian thinks it was a little boring. "They tried to make it more exciting with the Alien thing, but it wasn't enough to make the ride really fun."

Karyn disagrees. "No matter how many times I ride, I still love it. I really love old movies, but if they want to appeal to younger kids, they should update it so there are movies that they know. But I just think it's neat learning about old movies."

Ashley likes the ride just the way it is. "I like the ride a lot," she says. "I think it's interesting to see all the old movies, and I don't think they should make it more modern." The kids agree that the guide driving the vehicle has a lot to do with how much they like the trip. "The first time I really liked it," says Taran, "because the guide was good. The second time, she wasn't as good, so it was a little boring. I also think it would be better if you travel through a more modern movie."

Nita says, "I really like the ride,

PICTURE YOURSELF HERE

PICTURE YOURSELF HERE

79

but it does depend on the guide. I especially like when it gets windy as you go through the *Fantasia* scene and into *The Wizard of Oz*."

David has been on The Great Movie Ride a few times and thinks "it doesn't get boring. But I agree that they should have more modern movies."

Lissy thinks "it explains the movies really well and the characters look almost real. I like the songs, too."

Jim Henson's Muppet*Vision 3-D

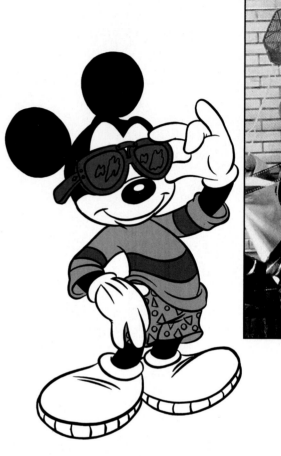

This is one of Walt Disney World's best attractions. It begins with a very funny pre-show starring Fozzie Bear, Gonzo, Bean Bunny, and Sam Eagle. Then you go into a specially designed theater. You see incredible 3-D effects mixed with some live special effects—so it's hard to tell what's part of the movie and what's real.

"The characters literally come right out at you," observes Lissy. "It's really cool that they have real things happening, so when they throw the pie you think it will be a real pie, too."

The real bubbles are a great special effect. "You really couldn't tell which were real and which were part of the movie," says Brian. "It's really more like 4-D."

Taran agrees. "The whole movie is in your face," he says. "I think it's awesome. I love when you get wet and when the bubbles come down, and I also love the little 3-D spirit, Waldo, because he seems like he's talking only to you."

Robert and Ashley feel the same way. "I thought the 3-D guy was just pointing at me. I can't believe

"The whole movie is in your face!"

—Taran (age 9)

" **You have to see it a few times to get all the jokes.** "

—Karyn (age 13)

he was pointing at everyone," says Robert. And Ashley says, "It looked like he was only looking at me. I leaned over to Karyn to see if he was looking at her, too."

Nita and Karyn have seen this attraction before. Nita reminds you to look at the back of the theater from time to time "because there's a lot of stuff happening back there and most people miss it, at least on their first visit."

Karyn says, "I just love this movie. You have to see it a few times to get all the jokes and appreciate more of the details, like the two guys sitting in the balcony. They're really funny."

SuperStar Television

This is your chance to star in a famous television show. Before going inside the SuperStar Television theater, members of the audience are chosen to appear in scenes from shows such as "I Love Lucy," "Cheers," "Home Improvement," or to hit a grand slam for the New York Mets. There are a lot of people chosen, but they don't pick too many kids. If you think you'd like to be a star, be sure to stand in the front and wave and make lots of noise.

Once inside, the people picked from the audience act out scenes and their pictures are blended with the real programs. Don't worry if you're camera shy or don't get picked. Watching is just as much fun as being on screen.

"I think it's cool that they let you participate, but you don't have to if you don't want to," says Lissy.

Karyn was chosen to be a New York Mets baseball player. "I really liked being in it, but I wish I could have seen it, too," she says. Karyn got to hit a homerun and then be

HOT TIP:

Make sure you stand in the front if you want to get picked for a part.

Love Lucy" scene with the chocolates on the conveyor belt. It's fun to see people from the audience play the roles of famous actors," says Brian.

"You can see it over and over again," says Nita, "because the scenes are different depending on who gets picked. It can be really funny when people goof up."

Taran's favorite part "is the David Letterman scene when he drops things off the Empire State Building." David says, "the show is neat. I like how they have the characters in just the right parts so it looks real."

interviewed by Howard Cosell.
The rest of the kids enjoyed watching. "My favorite is the "I

"I really liked being in it, but I wish I could have seen it, too."

—Karyn (age 13)

The Magic of Disney Animation

See how *Beauty and the Beast*, *Aladdin*, *The Little Mermaid*, and all the other Disney animated movies were created. And watch cartoon artists at work on future Disney hits, such as *The Lion King*.

In the waiting area of this attraction, there are displays of "cels" from famous movies. (A cel is the actual painted film used in the animated movie.) The Academy Awards that Walt Disney won for *Snow White and the Seven Dwarfs* also are on display.

When it's time for the show, you go into a theater to see a very funny movie starring Robin Williams and Walter Cronkite. Robin is turned into a cartoon to teach us how animated films are made. After the movie, you can walk through the animation studio and see artists at work. To find out more about what they're doing, just look at the screens overhead. Robin Williams and Walter Cronkite star again. This time they're explaining each step of the animation process. Try to see this

> ## "It's fun but you can learn at the same time."
> —Lissy (age 11)

show during the day since the animators usually go home about 6 P.M. The attraction usually doesn't open until 11 A.M.

All the kids like the way this attraction makes learning fun. "I think Robin Williams is so funny," says Lissy. "It's fun but you can learn at the same time." Ashley agrees. "I like how they had Robin Williams as the character," she says. "And I like how much you learn about animation."

This attraction is especially interesting to Brian, who is taking a class in cartoon drawing. "You can learn a lot by watching, and the movie is so funny," he says. "I like how you can see the real cels."

David finds it "fascinating to see all the cels that they really use in

the movies. I love that you can walk through and see real animators at work," he adds. "It's like taking your own personal tour."

Nita also likes the walking part of the tour the best. "Just watching the artists work is so interesting," she says.

Karyn likes that they take you step-by-step through the animation process. "It's just so neat to see how they make animated movies," she says.

> ## "It's just so neat to see how they make animated movies."
> —Karyn (age 13)

Honey, I Shrunk the Kids Movie Set Adventure

Honey, I Shrunk the Kids Movie Set Adventure Checklist

Bee Hive
Cheerios
Dog's Nose
Leaky Hose
Roll of Film Slide
Spider Web
Tree Slide
Underground Cave

The backyard in this popular movie has been re-created as an oversize playground. Even grown-ups feel small here. There are 30-foot-tall blades of grass, giant tree stumps, huge Lego toys, a big garden hose with a leak, and lots more. You have many places to explore and plenty of things to climb on and slide down.

"I think it looks more like honey, I blew up the garden, " says Taran. "It's really cool. I like the cave the best, but I advise you to take a friend because it's more fun with more people."

Robert likes it "because there are so many different places to go. This playground would never get boring for me."

Lissy thinks the "whole place is neat.

Not just the slides and the swings—there's a lot for older kids to notice, like all the things that look like they come straight from the movie."

Most of the kids enjoyed trying to get wet under the giant leaky hose. This is a real challenge since

> **"This playground would never get boring for me."**
>
> —Robert (age 8)

86

> "It looks more like honey, I blew up the garden!"
>
> —Taran (age 9)

water squirts from a different spot each time.

Some of the older kids prefer watching the younger kids in action and would like to bring a younger brother or sister to play. "I like the slides and the big net, but I think it's more for younger kids," says Brian.

Karyn agrees. "I'm the type of person who would just love to take a little kid around and watch them have fun."

"It's fun to jump around for a little while, but I think little kids would just love it," says David.

For parents, the playground is a place to take a little rest. We found that setting a meeting time at a certain spot worked great.

Backstage Studio Tour

There is a real working studio at the Disney-MGM Studios Theme Park. This tram ride takes you through parts of the backstage area where scenes from movies and television shows are filmed. Your trip includes Catastrophe Canyon, a great special effects show demonstrating an explosion, a fire, and a flash flood. You also get to see the costume department, the lighting department, and some of the props from famous movies.

"You learn something the whole time while still having fun," says Lissy. "I really like Catastrophe Canyon," she adds. "It shows that special effects are much safer than they look."

Robert agrees. "Catastrophe Canyon is really cool. When the explosions go off, it gets really hot. Then when the water comes down, it gets really cold. I also like the Delta plane a lot. The guide told us that the plane has been used in filming a lot of movies."

If you like getting wet, sit on the left side of the tram.

Brian thinks part of the tour is a little boring. "I loved the Catastrophe Canyon part, but I wasn't crazy about the rest," he says.

But Ashley enjoyed touring the back streets where "seeing the houses without the backs is cool.

"It shows that special effects are much safer than they look."

—Lissy (age 11)

They only shoot the front for the shows, so that's all they build," she points out.

"It's pretty cool how you get to go past the actual homes from some television shows," adds David. "I particularly liked seeing the Bulldog Café from the *Rocketeer*."

Taran is also interested in the back streets, but for a different reason. "Catastrophe Canyon is great, but I really like the movie props because I like building models," he says.

Nita has seen this attraction before. "I like this tour," she says, "but a lot depends on the guide. If you get a really good guide the tour is much better."

D. DUCK

Beauty and the Beast Stage Show

Belle, Gaston, Mrs. Potts, Chip, Lumiere, Cogsworth, and the Beast come to life in this musical show based on the hot movie. The show opens with "Be Our Guest." Then it backtracks to the beginning of the story, where Belle is unhappy in her small French town. Belle is held captive in the Beast's castle, and later he is attacked by all the townspeople. In the finale, Belle and the Beast declare their love and the wicked spell is broken.

"I especially love when the white doves fly out at the end," says Nita. "It adds so much to the scene. I also love the costumes and, of course, the music."

Karyn loves this show. "There are so many details, like the dancing dishes and spoons, and the costumes are so beautiful."

Some of the kids are not as enthusiastic. "I don't like that the show starts with "Be Our Guest" so the songs aren't in the same order as the movie," says Ashley. "I did like the costumes, though."

Robert agrees. "The songs should be in the same order as the movie. It's confusing," he says.

"It's weird the way the songs are mixed up, but I still like the costumes and the music." says Lissy. "The singing is really good."

Taran says, "I think if you loved the movie, you'll like this show, but I wasn't crazy about the movie."

All of the kids think that the

"The songs should be in the same order as in the movie."

—Robert (age 8)

90

> " I love all the costumes and, of course, the music. "
>
> —Nita (age 14)

fighting scene isn't very good. "The fighting parts don't look right, not like fighting at all," says David. Nita agrees. "I don't think little kids would get it that the dancers are supposed to be fighting," she says. "I know they are changing costumes during that scene, but it's so long."

What We Missed

We were able to see most of the attractions at the Studios during our one day there, but we did miss a few things. The **Inside the Magic Special Effects and Production Tour** is a behind-the-scenes look at different aspects of moviemaking. On this tour you see how some scenes from *Honey, I Shrunk the Kids* were filmed and how a battle scene at sea is shot. The tour takes you

through actual soundstages, so you may get to see a movie or a television show being filmed.

The **Voyage of The Little Mermaid** is a live show that features Ariel and Prince Eric. Flounder, Sebastian, and other characters from the movie are played by puppets. The puppeteers are dressed all in black, so it looks like the puppets are suspended in mid-air. There is a screen of water at the front of the stage that makes you feel like you're under the sea. The characters sing some songs from the movie. You also see a battle between the evil Ursula and Ariel, with some special effects like lasers and lightning. At the end, everyone lives happily ever after.

Don't be fooled by the name of the **Monster Sound Show**. There are no monsters in this show. Instead, audience members are chosen to participate in creating sound effects for a movie. One person is in charge of the doorbell, someone else takes care of the crashing chandelier, another person creates the sound of thunder. It shows how hard it is to make the sounds of movies happen at just the right time. It's fun to participate, so be sure to raise your hand. After the show, go into the area called

SoundWorks, where you can have some hands-on sound effects experiences.

Leonardo, Michelangelo, Donatello, and Raphael, those famous turtles from the sewers of New York, put on a show at the Studios. At the **Teenage Mutant Ninja Turtle Show**, the turtles perform their theme song and

then hang around for autographs.

Kermit, Miss Piggy, Fozzie Bear, Gonzo, and Bean Bunny, all stars of Muppet*Vision 3-D, pose for photos and sign autographs several times each day at **Jim Henson's Muppets on Location**. Dr. Teeth and the Electric Mayhem Band perform a few musical numbers.

AWESOME
(See at Least Twice)

Jim Henson's
Muppet*Vision 3-D

Star Tours

Indiana Jones
Stunt Spectacular

94

WAY COOL
(Don't Miss)

The Magic of
Disney
Animation

SuperStar
Television

COOL
(Check it Out)

Beauty and the Beast
Stage Show

The Great Movie Ride

Backstage Studio Tour

Honey, I Shrunk the Kids
Movie Set Adventure

My visit to Disney-MGM
Studios will include . . .

Indiana Jones S.S.
Star Tours
The Great Movie Ride
Muppet Vision 3-D
Super Star Television
The Magic of Disney A.
Backstage Studio Tour
Inside the Magic
Monster Sound Show

YAWN
(Save For Last)

Everything Else in the World

When most kids think about Walt Disney World, they think of the Magic Kingdom, Epcot Center, and the Disney-MGM Studios Theme Park. But as we discovered on our trip, there is much more to see.

There is a petting farm with lots of baby animals, a wooded campground with a water park known as River Country, an island where endangered species are cared for, another state-of-the-art water park called Typhoon Lagoon, lakes where you can rent boats, the Disney Village Marketplace, a behind-the-scenes program called Wonders of Walt Disney World, and lots of restaurants and hotels.

In this chapter you can read about all these extras and decide which ones you most want to see. The kids agree that making time for Discovery Island and renting Water Sprites for a ride on one of Walt Disney World's waterways are a great break from the theme park routine.

So read on and help your parents decide where to stay, where to eat, and which added attractions to visit.

DISCOVERY ISLAND

Discovery Island is the perfect place to spend a morning—or even a whole day—away from the theme parks. You can see many different types of birds, huge turtles, and several endangered species. It's like a natural zoo with lots of trees and plants, so you feel almost like you're in a forest. You can explore the island on your own by using the map you get when you arrive and by following the marked paths. Kids ages 8 to 14 can sign up for a Discovery Island Kidventure, a four-hour guided tour (see the box on the next page for details).

Besides looking at all the animals and plants, you can learn

"It's a place I could go to 100 times and never be bored."

—Robert

(age 8)

> "You can see animals that you would never see anywhere else."
>
> —Lissy (age 11)

Discovery Island Kidventure

If you think you'd like to explore Discovery Island with an expert, you can sign up for the four-hour tour that includes transportation, lunch, crafts materials, and a souvenir photo. The cost is $26.50. You must make a reservation in advance. The phone number for reservations is 407-824-3784.

about different products that are bad for the environment and harmful to endangered animals. And there's a hospital right on the island where injured animals are cared for. You can look in through glass windows and see the veterinarian at work.

The kids agree that Discovery Island should definitely be on your schedule. Most of them never even knew it existed. "I was surprised that this would be at Walt Disney World," says Lissy.

Along the paths you get to see birds that sound like other animals. "I like the barking swan and the bird that sounds like a croaking frog," says Ashley. "It's neat that that's how they protect their territory."

Nita likes the fact that "they take care of all the animals, even ones that don't belong there. The hospital is nice, too. It looks just like a real hospital," she says.

David thinks Discovery Island is a "great way to see these birds, maybe for the last time. They're

trying to save a lot of birds that are becoming extinct."

Robert thinks the whole island is great. "It's a place I could go to 100 times and never be bored," he says.

The kids got to see some animals up close, like a baby alligator, a hedgehog, and the huge turtles. "The hedgehog is pretty cute," says Ashley, "and the turtles are neat but they smell bad."

Lissy says that "you can see animals that you would never see anywhere else. It's so exotic," she says. "The place is just awesome."

97

FORT WILDERNESS

Tucked away in a wooded area of Walt Disney World is Fort Wilderness. There are many activities here, and some people actually stay in trailers in the woods. You can bring your own trailer from home or you can rent a furnished trailer as if it were a hotel room. There are a few pools, tennis courts, volleyball courts, hayrides, a huge marina with lots of boats, and a petting farm. River Country water park also is located here. It is described later in this chapter.

Fort Wilderness has so much to offer, you could spend days here without seeing everything. We had only a few hours, so we explored the petting farm and then we rented Water Sprites for a ride around Bay Lake.

Fort Wilderness Petting Farm

This small farm is home to some extra-friendly goats, several sheep, a donkey, rabbits, pigs, chickens, and a few other birds and animals, including ponies that you can ride.

The kids agree that the farm is great for younger children and fun for kids their own age, too. "The farm gives you a chance to get up close to the animals without being afraid of anything," says Lissy. Robert agrees. "I especially like letting the little baby goats chew on my fingers," he says.

Karyn remembers that she "used to love petting farms. But now it's a little boring. If you really like

Water Sprites

These small motor boats don't actually go very fast, but they feel like they do. With the wind whipping in your face and the nose of the boat lifting into the air, the sensation of speed is great. You must be at least 12 years old to drive a Water Sprite (with or without an adult). If you're under 12, you can ride as a passenger with a parent or an older brother or sister. The kids in our group who are under 12 rode with the older kids instead of with an adult.

The Water Sprite trip gets very high marks from all the kids. The rental is for 30 minutes, and you can cover a large portion of Bay Lake in that time. You can even make a trip around Discovery Island. Water Sprites can be rented at some other locations. See the end of this section for details.

"It's awesome," says Brian. "I was turning into the waves and one splashed on top of me."

David thinks being able to drive your own boat is neat. "I love going over the water. This is fun at Fort Wilderness that you definitely can't miss," he adds. Lissy thinks the Water Sprites are "loads of fun, and being in the water really cools you off."

animals, though, it would never be boring no matter how old you are." Brian agrees. "I recommend this place for anyone who loves animals," he says.

Where to Rent Water Sprites

Water Sprites also can be rented at the *Contemporary Resort*, the *Polynesian Resort*, the *Grand Floridian Resort*, and the Disney Village Marketplace. The cost is $11 for a half-hour. If you happen to be staying at the *Caribbean Beach Resort* (and you're at least 10 years old) you can rent a Toobie, which is an oversize inner tube with a motor. Toobies offer the same type of ride as Water Sprites.

Karyn likes the scenery around the lake. "It's fun to go all around Discovery Island because it's really pretty with all the trees."

Some of the kids think the boats should go faster, but Nita says "it's not too fast and not too slow."

More Fun at Fort Wilderness

There are many other activities available at Fort Wilderness. You can rent a canoe ($4 per hour or $9 per day) for a trip along the canals around the campground. Or you can rent a bicycle ($3 per hour or $7 per day) and explore one of the many trails. At the Horse Barn, you can see the champion Percherons that pull the trolleys down Main Street in the Magic Kingdom. Sometimes the blacksmith is there to answer questions about the special shoes he makes for the horses. There are hayrides that last about an hour and cost $3 for kids and $5 for adults. It's also possible to go on an organized fishing trip, or just to fish in the canals.

WATERS OF THE WORLD

Walt Disney World is a water wonderland. With two spectacular water parks and unique swimming pools at the resorts, getting wet, staying cool, and having fun at Walt Disney World is very easy. Because we visited Walt Disney World in February, the weather was very cool (in the high 50s), so we weren't able to go swimming. But here is a description of water parks and some of the special pools so you can decide which you'd like to try out most.

Typhoon Lagoon

This watery playground is a great place to spend a whole day. The surf lagoon is larger than two football fields, and the four-and-a-half-foot waves make body surfing fun. There are two speed slides that send you though a cave at 30 miles per hour, a couple of winding storm

102

Arrive at Typhoon Lagoon when it opens or else wait until late afternoon.

slides, and a whitewater slide that gives groups and families a chance to ride the rapids together. There's also a special area just for younger children called Ketchakiddie Creek, which has smaller slides and other games.

On top of Mount Mayday, the mountain in the center of Typhoon Lagoon, there is a boat called the *Miss Tilly*. Keep an eye on the smokestack on top of the boat. It shoots a flume of water every five or ten minutes. If you climb all the way to the top of Mount Mayday, you get a great view of all the activities at Typhoon Lagoon.

The biggest and fastest water slides are called Humunga Cowabunga. Castaway Creek is a stream that circles the entire park. You can hop in an oversize tube and float around Castaway Creek. There are lots of props along the way, and you can get in and out of the creek at many locations.

There also are volleyball courts, a shop, two restaurants, and lots of lounge chairs for your parents.

River Country

If you've ever read *The Adventures of Tom Sawyer* and *The Adventures of Huckleberry Finn*, River Country will seem like it came right from those stories. Disney Imagineers have created a swimming hole just like the ones Tom and Huck used to visit—only this one is much bigger. It has a huge swimming pool with two steep water slides. The main section of River Country is Bay Cove, an area with rope swings, a ship's boom, and other things made for swinging and jumping into the water. Bay Cove also has two flume rides that send you down a corkscrew path into the water.

Other River Country activities include a whitewater ride in a large inner tube, an area for younger kids with smaller slides and water toys to play with, and a small beach. There also is a snack stand.

Hotel Pools

There are some great pools at the Walt Disney World resorts. You are allowed to swim in the

Where To Get Wet in the Theme Parks

There are several attractions around the three major parks that offer chances to get wet. At the Magic Kingdom, try Splash Mountain (especially if you sit in the front row). At Epcot Center, you can spend hours playing at the jumping fountains outside the Journey Into Imagination Pavilion. At the Disney-MGM Studios Theme Park, the Backstage Studio Tour provides a splash during Catastrophe Canyon (sit on the left for a wetter ride), and the leaky hoses at the Honey, I Shrunk the Kids Movie Set Adventure playground spurt water unexpectedly.

pools only if you are a guest of the hotel. So read this section carefully, and then read the rest of the hotel information later in this chapter. Then you can give your parents advice on where you'd most like to stay.

One of the best pools is Stormalong Bay at the *Yacht and Beach Club* resorts. There is a sunken ship with a built-in water slide so you can climb the wreck and slide back down to the water. At *Port Orleans*, Doubloon Lagoon is a pool built around a sea serpent that may still be lingering underground. His tail can be seen jutting up in spots along the walkways, and the water slide is actually the serpent's tongue. Ol' Man Island is a three-and-a-half-acre recreation center at *Dixie Landings.* It features a large themed pool with slides and ropes. At the *Polynesian* resort, the Swimming Pool Lagoon is surrounded by a large cluster of boulders that actually are a water slide. The Grotto Pool between the *Dolphin* and *Swan* hotels is a group of connecting pools with bridges and a water slide.

RESTAURANT GUIDE

There are so many restaurants at Walt Disney World that you should have no trouble finding someplace you like. To help you sort through the choices, here are our recommendations for the best eating spots for kids. Remember, this is not a complete listing of all the restaurants at Walt Disney World.

When you plan your day, look at this list and choose a restaurant near where you expect to be at mealtime. Then read through the selections to find a place that serves food you like. The key below explains the letters and dollar signs at the end of each listing. The letters tell you which meals are served. The dollar signs give you an idea of how much your meal will cost. If a restaurant has the letter "B" at the end of its listing, a full breakfast is offered there.

B reakfast
L unch
D inner
S nacks
$ Inexpensive
$$ Moderate
$$$ Expensive

MAGIC KINGDOM

Waitress Service

Diamond Horseshoe Jamboree: Frontierland. Sandwiches, chips. Western entertainment. $. L, S.

King Stefan's Banquet Hall: Fantasyland. Prime ribs, seafood, beef, chicken, salads. $$$. L, D.

Liberty Tree Tavern: Liberty Square. Seafood, chicken, beef, sandwiches, salads. $$$. L, D.

Tony's Town Square: Main Street. Pizza, spaghetti with meatballs, burgers with toppings. $$. B, L, D.

Fast Food

Adventureland Veranda: Adventureland. Oriental specials, burgers, hot dogs. $. L, D, S.

Aunt Polly's Landing: Tom Sawyer Island. Cold fried chicken, ham and cheese sandwiches, peanut-butter-and-jelly, soft-serve ice cream, lemonade. $. L, S.

Columbia Harbour House: Liberty Square. Seafood, chicken, salads. $. L, D, S.

Crystal Palace: Main Street. Cafeteria: pasta, hot dogs, fish, chicken, salads. $$. B, L, D, S.

Lumiere's Kitchen: Fantasyland. Chicken nuggets, grilled cheese, cookies. $. L, D, S.

Pecos Bill Café: Frontierland. Burgers, barbecued chicken sandwiches, hot dogs. $. L, D, S.

Pinocchio Village Haus: Fantasyland. Burgers, hot dogs, sandwiches, salads. $. L, D, S.

Tomorrowland Terrace: Tomorrowland. Soups, salads, sandwiches, ice cream. $. L, D, S.

Snack Spots

Liberty Square Market: Liberty Square. Fresh fruit. $. S.

Lunching Pad: Tomorrowland. Frozen yogurt, fresh fruit. $. S.

Plaza Ice Cream Parlor: Main Street. Lots of flavors. $. S.

Round Table: Fantasyland. Soft-serve sundaes, floats. $. S.

Pure & Simple: Wonders of Life. Sandwiches, salads, waffles, frozen yogurt, juices. $. L, S.
Stargate: CommuniCore East. Burgers, chicken sandwiches, hot dogs, salads, soft-serve ice cream. $. B, L, D, S.
Sunrise Terrace: CommuniCore West. Pizza, pasta. $. L, D, S.

World Showcase

Waitress Service

Au Petit Café: France. Sautéed chicken fingers, pasta, ground beef steaks. $$ to $$$. L, D, S.
Biergarten: Germany. Chicken, frankfurters, sausages, potato pancakes. $$ to $$$. L, D.
L'Originale Alfredo di Roma Ristorante: Italy. Fettucine Alfredo, pasta, chicken, veal. $$$. L, D.
Marrakesh: Morocco. Chicken, bastila (cinnamon chicken pastry), sampler platters. $$$. L, D.
San Angel Inn: Mexico. Chicken, beef, guacamole, tacos. $$$. L, D.
Teppanyaki Dining Rooms: Japan. Stir-fried meat, vegetables, fish cooked at the table. $$$. L, D.

Fast Food

Cantina de San Angel: Mexico. Burritos, tortillas with chicken and refried beans. $. L, D.
Kringla Bakeri og Kafe: Norway. Sandwiches, pastries. $. L, S.

Sunshine Tree Terrace: Adventureland. Orange slush, frozen yogurt shakes. $. S.
Westward Ho: Frontierland. Cookies, pretzels, chips. $. S.

EPCOT CENTER
Future World

Waitress Service

Coral Reef: Living Seas. Seafood, pasta, chicken. $$$. L, D.
The Land Grille Room: The Land. Chicken, steaks, sandwiches, seafood, pizza. $$ to $$$. B, L, D.

Fast Food

Farmers Market: The Land. Food court. $. L, D, S.
Odyssey: Near Mexico. Chicken sandwiches, burgers, hot dogs, salads. $. L, D, S.

Liberty Inn: The American Adventure. Burgers, hot dogs, chili, chicken sandwiches, French fries. $ to $$. L, D, S.
Lotus Blossom Café: China. Sweet-and-sour pork, stir-fried beef, egg rolls, soup. $. L, D.
Sommerfest: Germany. Bratwurst sandwiches, soft pretzels, apple strudel. $. L, D, S.
Yakitori House: Japan. Yakitori (skewered chicken), teriyaki sandwiches. $. L, D, S.

Snack Spots

Boulangerie Pâtisserie: France. Pastries, croissants, éclairs, chocolate mousse. $. S.
Refreshment Outpost: Between Germany and China. Frozen yogurt, cookies, fresh fruit. $. S.
Refreshment Port: Canada. Frozen yogurt, cookies, fruit. $. S.

Eating Healthy

Most restaurants, including fast-food stands, now have a lot more healthy foods such as salads, fresh fruit, broiled or grilled chicken breasts, turkey burgers, and nonfat frozen yogurt.

DISNEY-MGM STUDIOS THEME PARK

Waitress Service

50's Prime Time Café: Macaroni and cheese, burgers, tuna salad sandwiches, chicken pot pie, hot roast beef, alphabet soup, ice cream sodas, shakes. $$. L, D, S.
Mama Melrose's Ristorante Italiano: Pizza, lasagna, meatball subs, chicken, pasta. $$ to $$$. L, D (dinner only offered seasonally).
Sci-Fi Dine-In Theater: Burgers, pasta, salads. $$ to $$$. L, D.

Fast Food

Backlot Express: Chicken, burgers, hot dogs, salads. $. L, D, S.
Disney-MGM Studios Commissary: Chicken salad, stir-fry, sandwiches, teriyaki burgers. $. L, D.

Food Courts

Food courts make it easy to satisfy everyone in your family at mealtimes. We tried Old Port Royale at the *Caribbean Beach* resort. Its six counters serve everything from pizza and pasta to burgers, sandwiches, and Chinese food. For dessert, there is a bakery that also serves ice cream. The kids like being able to choose their own meals. Brian says, "There are a lot of good things to eat. I love all the selections." Ashley agrees. "I especially like the pizza," she says.

Other hotel food courts are at *Port Orleans* and *Dixie Landings*. At the theme parks, you'll find the *Farmers Market* in the Land Pavilion of Epcot Center, and the *Soundstage* at the Disney-MGM Studios Theme Park.

Hollywood & Vine "Cafeteria of the Stars": Chicken, spaghetti and meatballs, tortellini, ribs, salads. $$. B, L, D.
Soundstage: Food court with *Aladdin* setting. $. L, D.

Snack Spots
Dinosaur Gertie's: Ice cream bars and sandwiches, fruit yogurt bars, frozen bananas. $. S.
Studio Catering Company: Fresh fruit, sundaes, milk shakes. $. S.

109

Eating With the Characters

Kids of all ages enjoy having breakfast with the characters—especially since it's so easy to have your picture taken with them. David thinks "seeing all the Disney characters joke and dance around makes breakfast very special." Below is a list of where you can eat breakfast with the characters. To check reservation policies call 407-W-DISNEY.

Contemporary Café,
   Contemporary
Cape May Café,
   Beach Club
Papeete Bay, Polynesian
1900 Park Fare, Grand Floridian
   (Characters also entertain at
   dinner.)
Ristorante Carnivale, Dolphin
Garden Grove, Swan

Other restaurants where you can eat with the characters include: the *Empress Lilly* and *Chef Mickey's Village Restaurant* in Disney Village Marketplace, *King Stefan's Banquet Hall* in The Magic Kingdom, *Stargate* and *Odyssey* in Epcot Center, and *Soundstage* in the Disney-MGM Studios Theme Park.

Hot Tip: Ask about portion sizes if you don't order from the kids menu or you may get way too much food.

Eating at the Hotels

Most of the Walt Disney World resorts have several restaurants. Here is our list of the best spots in each hotel for kids.

Contemporary:	Contemporary Café
Polynesian:	Papeete Bay Verandah
Disney Inn:	Disney Inn Restaurant
Grand Floridian:	1900 Park Fare
Dixie Landings:	Colonel's Cotton Mill Food Court
Port Orleans:	Sassagoula Floatworks Food Court
Caribbean Beach:	Old Port Royale Food Court
Disney Vacation Club:	Olivia's Café
Yacht and Beach Club:	Beaches & Cream Soda Shop
Dolphin:	Coral Café
Swan:	Garden Grove Café
Fort Wilderness:	Trail's End Buffeteria

Kid Favorites

Although almost every restaurant at Walt Disney World caters to kids, our group definitely had its favorites. Among them was *Ristorante Carnivale* at the *Dolphin*. Brian says, "The food is delicious, and while you wait there is entertainment. They have jugglers and singers who tell jokes. It's a really fun place to be." David agrees. "The waiters are very amusing," he says.

For a quick bite, try *Pecos Bill Café* in the Magic Kingdom. Karyn says, "The Wild West setting is fun, and the food is great." Taran agrees. "My chicken sandwich was awesome, and we got the food fast," he says. Robert points out that "you have a great view of the Walt Disney World Railroad, Splash Mountain, and the other sights in Frontierland."

Another choice for a quick meal is *Odyssey* in Epcot Center. Taran says that "the food was fast and we had a great time." Nita agrees, but mentions that "it's more fun when the characters are there. They come to your table while you eat." Karyn prefers this restaurant for "a quick bite to eat when you don't want to take a lot of time."

GUEST CHECK

Restaurants I'd like to go to:
Sci-Fi Dine-In

how the waitresses and waiters pretend to be Mom and Dad." Nita thinks this is the best choice for both parents and kids. "No matter how old you are, you can become a kid at the *50's Prime Time Café,*" she says.

OTHER RESTAURANTS RECOMMENDED FOR KIDS:

At *Chef Mickey's Village Restaurant* in Disney Village Marketplace, you can meet Mickey Mouse. Lissy says that "meeting Chef Mickey is fun." Nita seconds. "I would tell others about this place," she says.

The kids agree that the *50's Prime Time Café* at the Disney-MGM Studios Theme Park is their top choice. David says, "I have never had so much fun in a restaurant in my entire life." Ashley agrees, "I love the entertainment," she says. Lissy thinks "it's so neat

Magic Kingdom

Tony's Town Square
King Stephan's Banquet Hall
Aunt Polly's Landing
Lumiere's Kitchen

Epcot Center

Liberty Inn
L'Originale Alfredo di Roma
 Ristorante
Biergarten

Disney-MGM Studios Theme Park

Sci-Fi Dine-In Theater
Soundstage

Snack Wagons

All around the theme parks are wagons that sell soft drinks, popcorn, and lots of ice cream—Cookies 'n' Cream ice cream sandwiches, Mouseketeer Bars, lowfat strawberry yogurt, and strawberry bars.
Some wagons now offer fresh fruit, too.

WALT DISNEY WORLD RESORTS

T here are 13 resorts all around the Walt Disney World property. Two more resorts will open during the summer of 1994. That means there are enough rooms at Walt Disney World for you to stay in a different spot every night for almost 37 years!

During our visit, we stayed at the *Dolphin* hotel. Everyone agrees that the *Dolphin* is a good choice for kids. There are six restaurants and an ice cream parlor, a gameroom, two pools, boat rentals, four shops, and Camp *Dolphin*, a special program just for kids.

"The *Dolphin* is very colorful and I like the way they treat kids," says Nita. Ashley agrees. "Camp Dolphin is great and the rooms are very nice," she says.

We visited some of the other resorts during our stay, including the *Contemporary*, the *Polynesian*, the *Disney Vacation Club*, and the *Caribbean Beach*.

Here are brief descriptions of the hotels we visited, plus the rest of the resorts at Walt Disney World.

There's information on the things that are most important to kids like gamerooms, special programs, restaurants, and recreational activities. For more details about the pools at each hotel, see pages 103 and 104.

Contemporary: The monorail rides through the center of this modern-style hotel. There are two restaurants, two pools, a playground, boat rentals, seven shops, and a huge gameroom. "If you love to play video games, you'll love this place," says Ashley.

113

Lissy agrees. "The gameroom is huge and awesome," she says. The kids also like that the monorail travels right through the building.

Polynesian: The decor here looks like it comes straight from the South Seas, with beautiful plants and trees all around. There are three restaurants, two pools, a playground, boat rentals, a gameroom, and six shops. "The Polynesian has a beautiful beach," says Brian. Karyn thinks "it's a nice and relaxing place to stay." Nita and David like the pool with its big slide.

Grand Floridian: At first glance, this elegant hotel seems to be designed for grown-ups only, but there are lots of things for kids to do, too. There is one pool, boat rentals, a playground, a gameroom, and four shops.

Disney Inn: This is a very quiet hotel located near some of the Walt Disney World golf courses. There is one restaurant, three pools, a small gameroom, and two shops.

Caribbean Beach: The rooms at this hotel are located in many very colorful buildings. There is one main pool, plus five other smaller pools, a food court with six counter restaurants, boat and bicycle rentals, a playground, a small gameroom, and one shop. "It's a pretty hotel because of all the colors on the roofs," says Nita. Ashley agrees. "I think it's pretty cool. There is a nice pool and the rooms are nice, too."

Yacht and Beach Club: There are really two hotels here that connect in the center. One has a boating theme and the other has a beach theme. There is a large main pool, plus two smaller ones, five restaurants and an ice cream parlor, boat rentals, a gameroom, and two shops.

Swan: The Swan and the Dolphin are similar because they were designed as sister hotels by the same architect. The Swan has three restaurants, two pools, boat rentals, a small gameroom, Camp Swan (a children's program), and one shop.

Port Orleans: The special details at this hotel make it look like the city it's named for, New Orleans. There is one restaurant and a food court with six counter spots, a large specially designed pool, boat and bicycle rentals, a gameroom, and a shop.

Dixie Landings: Next door to Port Orleans, this hotel represents the countryside surrounding New Orleans. There is one restaurant and a food court with six counters, a large pool on a recreation island, plus five more pools, boat and bicycle rentals, a gameroom, and a shop.

Disney Vacation Club: The townhouses that make up this resort are more like homes. There are two restaurants, one main pool, plus smaller pools around the resort, a small gameroom, boat and bicycle rentals, and a shop. There is a VCR in the rooms and you can see movies and other videotapes for free. "It's like a regular townhouse," says Ashley. Karyn thinks it "would be a nice place to stay for a while because it's so homey."

Disney's Village Resort: There are several types of villas at Walt Disney World, ranging from one-bedroom suites to four-bedroom houses. There is one restaurant in the villa area, six pools, boat and bicycle rentals, and several small gamerooms.

Fort Wilderness Campground: Guests can either camp with their own equipment or rent a trailer home at this wooded campground. There are two restaurants, two pools, a large beach, boat and bicycle rentals, a petting farm, pony rides, two gamerooms, and two shops.

SHOPPING

It's easy to get overwhelmed by the number of shops and souvenirs at Walt Disney World. Shopping is an important part of your vacation, but you should decide in advance how much you can spend and how many souvenirs you can afford.

Most kids bring some of their own money for shopping. Whether you're spending your own money or your parents', be careful not to buy the first thing that catches your eye. You're bound to see something you like better later on. If you see a souvenir on your first day, write down the name of the shop where you saw it and how much it cost. Then you can always go back for it.

Here are some suggestions for souvenirs in several price ranges.

Under $5

Buttons	$ 1.00
Magnets	$ 1.25
Pins	$ 1.50
Keychains	$ 3.50
Posters	$ 3.95
WDW calendars	$ 3.99
Mousketeer ears	$ 4.95

Under $10

Character banks	$ 5.95
Baseball caps	$ 5.95
Minnie ears	$ 6.98
Waist pouches	$ 8.95
Mickey gloves	$ 9.95

Under $20

Plush characters	$10.95
Figment hats	$10.95
Plush hats	$14.95
Tote bags	$14.95
"M" baseball caps	$14.95
Clocks	$15.00
Videos	$19.95

Under $25

Sweatshirts	$22.00
Plush characters	$22.95
Clocks	$24.00

ENTERTAINMENT

There's always live entertainment going on at Walt Disney World. When you arrive in each theme park, pick up an entertainment schedule so you can decide what you want to see. Here are descriptions of some of the best shows.

Hoop-Dee-Doo Musical Revue

While you eat a dinner of fried chicken, ribs, and corn-on-the-cob, a group of entertainers who sing, dance, and tell jokes puts on a great show. "I really like the entertainment," says Ashley. David thinks the show is "very funny. I

was laughing the whole time." Robert says he would recommend it to anyone.

IllumiNations

A spectacular laser, water, and fireworks show takes place each night at Epcot Center around World Showcase Lagoon. The best spot to see it is on the little island between The American Adventure and Italy. "The lights, lasers, and fireworks are really cool," says Lissy. Karyn thinks the show "never gets old no matter how many times you see it."

SpectroMagic

This parade makes its way down Main Street in the Magic Kingdom twice each night during busy seasons. The advanced technology uses holograms, special lighting, and a state-of-the-art sound system.

Fireworks

During busy seasons when the parks are open late, there are spectacular fireworks shows at the Magic Kindgom and the Disney-MGM Studios Theme Park.

WONDERS OF THE WORLD

Kids ages 10 through 15 who are interested in the environment, art, or entertainment can sign up for a six-hour backstage learning adventure. There are three programs to choose from.

Wildlife Adventure: Exploring the Environment takes you on a safari through the Walt Disney World conservation area. There are discussions about wildlife identification, ecosystems, and environmental issues. You can observe alligators, vultures, snakes, and other creatures in their natural habitat.

Art Magic: Bringing Illusion to Life shows how artists at Walt Disney World create the illusion of reality in movies and the theme parks. This adventure includes a behind-the-scenes look at the animation process. You get to visit the Animation Production Floor and talk with an artist from Walt Disney Animation. You then learn about the use of theme, color, and forced perspective. The day concludes with a hands-on experience where you learn tips on drawing Disney characters.

Show Biz Magic: The Walt Disney World of Entertainment introduces you to the wide range of entertainment at Walt Disney World. Discussions on communication, show preparation, auditions, being a good audience, and star qualities are reinforced through talks with performers. Highlights of this adventure include a a trip into the tunnel system beneath the Magic Kingdom.

The cost is $75 for each program and you receive admission to the theme parks and backstage areas during each program, lunch, and a personalized certificate of completion. For reservations, call 407-354-1855.

Hot Tips

In this chapter, we'll give you advice on how to get the most out of your Walt Disney World trip. There are lots of planning suggestions, plus hints on making schedules, getting along with your parents, and some other tips the kids discovered on our trip. You may want to take notes as you go along since there's a lot to remember. There also is a glossary of the Disney lingo used in this book. So read on for some hot tips from the kids for the most awesome vacation in the World!

Turn the page for lots of hot tips!

GETTING READY TO GO

When to Go

Deciding when to visit Walt Disney World can be confusing. Karyn warns that "you can't do anything when it's really crowded." Nita says, "If you're not a person who likes crowds, go during the winter, because in the summer every line is long for everything." Brian agrees. "Definitely don't go during a holiday when school is off."

To avoid crowds, try to visit during the first two weeks in December. The weather is nice, and you can see all the Christmas shows and decorations. If the only time you can visit is during a school vacation or in the summer, allow plenty of extra time and plan your days carefully so you don't spend your entire vacation in line.

During the less crowded times, especially in January, attractions may be closed down for renovations.

Making a Schedule

The kids agree that you should definitely make a schedule. Karyn says, "The schedule doesn't have to be that detailed, just planned out so you basically know what you want to do. I would use this guide to plan out the whole time before leaving home."

Ashley suggests that "you read the guide and then sit down with your parents and see what everyone else wants to do." Nita agrees. "Work with your parents on the schedule, so you all get to do the things you want to do." Robert advises that "the book is your best tour guide because it

tells you about all the rides. If it says the Haunted Mansion is scary and you don't like scary rides, then you don't have to go on it."

First you should decide how many days to spend in each park. The kids agree that the ideal trip would last about ten days. They also agree that the minimum amount of time is about five days. You need at least two days for the Magic Kingdom, two days for Epcot Center, and a full day for the Disney-MGM Studios Theme Park.

Karyn suggests "including a day of swimming and relaxing, because if you're tired it's no fun.

Don't try to do everything at once. Plan a long, relaxed vacation and have fun." On hot days, it's a good idea to leave the parks, get your hand stamped, and go back to the hotel for lunch or to take a swim.

Plan each day by choosing the best time to see each attraction. To avoid the longest lines, follow the advice in the theme park tips on the next page. Try to be flexible, and allow extra time in the schedule for surprises.

Later in this section on page 124, there is some space for you to begin writing your family's schedule.

Packing Tips

When you pack, make sure you're prepared for either warm or cool weather. Layers are a good idea, so you can take something off if you get hot. You don't need dressy clothes unless your parents want to go to one of the fancy restaurants. Shorts or jeans and T-shirts are fine for just about everywhere. Here's a list to get you started:

- This book.
- Activities to keep you busy on the plane or in the car—books, magazines, puzzles, or hand-held video games.
- A sweatshirt or sweater.
- Shorts and jeans.
- Long-sleeved and short-sleeved shirts.
- Bathing suits.
- Broken-in sneakers or shoes.
- Sunscreen and a hat.

" **Be prepared for a lot of walking.** "

—Robert (age 8)

EPCOT CENTER TIPS

- Start your day at the Wonders of Life Pavilion, where you'll want to get on Body Wars and see Cranium Command first thing in the morning.
- Head over to World Showcase after Wonders of Life, and save the rest of Future World for the afternoon.
- Buy a passport at any World Showcase shop and get it stamped at every country. It's a great reminder of your trip.
- Don't miss the Serpentine Fountains outside the Journey Into Imagination Pavilion, where streams of water jump from fountain to fountain.
- The best place to watch IllumiNations is from the little island between Italy and the American Adventure.

MAGIC KINGDOM TIPS

- You won't have to wait in long lines if you go to Space Mountain, Splash Mountain, Big Thunder Mountain, Pirates of the Caribbean, the Jungle Cruise, and most of the Fantasyland attractions either first thing in the morning or during the 3 P.M. parade.
- If there are two lines, the one on the left is almost always shorter.
- Save time for shopping on Main Street.
- Never eat before riding Space Mountain.

If you want to see an attraction more than once, try it again at dusk when lines are usually shorter.

122

DISNEY-MGM STUDIOS THEME PARK TIPS

• Arrive at the Disney-MGM Studios Theme Park before the posted opening time. The gates usually open about 8:30 A.M.
• At the Honey, I Shrunk the Kids Movie Set Adventure playground, hang around the dog's nose and you'll get a surprise.
• Make sure to check the Studios Tip Board at the end of Hollywood Boulevard. It tells you which attractions are about to begin a new show, and which have the shortest lines.
• Get a good spot along Hollywood Boulevard to see Aladdin's Royal Caravan.
• When Tower of Terror opens in June, it will have very long lines. See it early in the day and never right after a meal.

Where the Lines Are

Here's a list of rides that often have long lines. Some of them are worth a long wait. Others should be saved for another time.

Rides Worth the Wait
Space Mountain
Splash Mountain
Big Thunder Mountain Railroad
Pirates of the Caribbean
Cranium Command
Body Wars
Jim Henson's Muppet*Vision 3-D
The Magic of Disney Animation
Star Tours
Beauty and the Beast Stage Show

Save for Another Time
20,000 Leagues Under the Sea
Dumbo, The Flying Elephant
It's A Small World
Mad Tea Party
Jungle Cruise
Country Bear Jamboree
Delta Dreamflight
Spaceship Earth Show
Journey Into Imagination Ride
Voyage of the Little Mermaid

My Visit to Walt Disney World

Day 1

Day 2

Day 3

Day 4

Day 5

TRAVELING WITH YOUR PARENTS (and brothers and sisters)

If you follow our hints for working out a schedule with your parents and brothers and sisters before you go, it will be easier to include something for everyone.

Remember that your parents are looking forward to this vacation as much as you are. Lissy warns, "Don't try to force your parents to do things that will make them unhappy because they will act unhappy." But don't worry, as Nita says, "no matter how old you are, you'll always love Disney World."

Here are a few hints to help everyone get along:

• Go to the most popular attractions early in the day so you don't have to argue about waiting in long lines. To ride the most popular attractions a second time, wait until during a parade or dusk, when the rides will be less crowded.

• At the Magic Kingdom, Tom Sawyer Island is a great spot where kids can climb hills and explore paths while parents take a break.

• Your parents will want to see the movies in World Showcase at Epcot Center. Plan your day so you begin at the Wonders of Life Pavilion with Body Wars and Cranium Command, and then head for the countries with the movies. Try not to see them all in a row. Remember, you have to stand for the movies in Canada and China. You get to sit down for the France movie. A good way to break up the movies is to go on the boat ride at Norway.

• Talk your parents into taking a break for ice cream or another snack in the late afternoon. Everyone gets tired of walking, so a cool snack is refreshing.

• The kids agree that Walt Disney World is more fun when you are there with other kids. Bring younger brothers and sisters (ages 2 to 7) to the Magic Kingdom. They'll really like Mickey's Starland; Dumbo, The Flying Elephant; It's A Small World; Cinderella's Golden Carrousel; and the Country Bear Jamboree. For younger kids who might be afraid of the dark, avoid Snow White's Adventures, Mr. Toad's Wild Ride, Peter Pan's Flight, Pirates of the Caribbean, and especially the Haunted Mansion. The kids also agree they'd like to play with younger siblings at the Honey, I Shrunk the Kids Movie Set Adventure playground at the Disney-MGM Studios Theme Park.

• If you're an older kid, you might want to split up from your parents for a while. Agree on a meeting time and place, and be sure you don't get in any long lines too close to your set time.

• If you turn around and your parents have disappeared, or if they don't show up at your agreed-upon meeting place, you should go to Baby Services or City Hall in the Magic Kingdom, Earth Station or Baby Services next to the *Odyssey* restaurant in Epcot Center, or Guest Services at the Disney-MGM Studios Theme Park.

TIPS FOR TAKING PICTURES

• In each park there are Photo Spots marked by little signs with cameras on them. Photos taken from these spots will come out best.

• It's fun to bring your own disposable camera. They're easy to use and carry, and this way you'll have your own pictures to paste in this book as a memory of your trip.

• Make sure your fingers aren't in front of the lens.

• Don't shoot too close or too far away from your subject.

• You cannot take pictures inside the attractions.

• Your parents will probably take lots of pictures of you with the characters. It would be fun to take pictures of *them* with their favorite characters.

PASTE
YOUR
FAVORITE
WALT DISNEY WORLD
PHOTO
HERE

WHERE TO FIND THE CHARACTERS

Check the entertainment schedule in each theme park so you can catch the character shows throughout the day.

Magic Kingdom: The characters appear next to City Hall during the day. There's an organized line so everyone gets a turn to meet the characters and have a photo taken. The best place to see the characters is Mickey's Starland where Mickey, Goofy, Bonkers, Baloo, Louie, and Dark Wing Duck are in a show. Then you can wait in line to get a picture with Mickey at the Hollywood Theater.

Epcot Center: At the *Odyssey* restaurant there are a few shows each day. The characters sing, dance, and stop at each table so you can get some great pictures. Also, the characters are often out in front of the pavilions in World Showcase, wearing costumes from each country.

Disney-MGM Studios Theme Park: Strolling down Mickey Avenue in mid-afternoon, you'll find very few people and many characters, so you can get lots of pictures. Also, Aladdin, Jasmine, the Genie, and Jafar walk around inside and outside the *Soundstage* restaurant.

Glossary

Audio-Animatronics: Lifelike figures, from birds and hippos to movie stars and presidents. They seem so alive that it's sometimes hard to tell which are the real thing and which are not.

Buffeteria: The Disney word for cafeteria.

Cel: The actual painted film used in an animated movie.

Disney Handwich: Bread cones with a variety of fillings so you can easily eat them using only one hand.

Imagineer: The Disney name for a creative engineer who designs theme park attractions.